EMPOWERING THE

INDIGENOUS

The DOULOS Story

David M. Johnson

With

Joshua B. Clarke

10/40 Window graphic used with permission from GBM.

Images were taken by Doulos Partners while in the field.

Details in some stories have been changed for the protection of the persons involved.

Edited by Anne Riley
Cover design: Uptick Marketing with images from Reaching Souls.

ISBN-13: 978-1722301699
ISBN-10: 1722301694

Printed in the United States of America.

All proceeds from the sale of this book go to support the work of indigenous church planters to reach their countrymen for Christ.

This book is dedicated to the
men and women around the world
who are sacrificially giving their lives
to tell others about Jesus.

Acknowledgements

Thank you to Glenn Parker for your consistent encouragement over the years to put into writing what God has done through Doulos Partners.

To Benjamin Francis, Jeff Gibson, and Brent Parsons, thank you for your time in helping gather updated information from our brothers in the field. Your hard work has enabled us to share their stories of how the Lord has transformed them and to hear how they are changing the world for Christ.

A special thank you to our editing team: Courtney Clarke, Susan Johnson, Glenn Parker, Anne Riley, and Bethany Timothy. This group worked tirelessly to ensure that the contents of this book were written in a way that was worth reading.

To Scott Gurosky and Wayne Myrick, thank you for listening when the Lord began to speak so many years ago and for taking time to write down your story as a part of this project.

Thank you to Paul Head for helping go through the board minutes and original paperwork to ensure that all of the dates and information were correct.

From David: Thank you to my bride, Susan, for your encouragement, understanding, and hard work on this project. It was such a blessing for me to work side by side with you to tell some of what the Lord has done over the last 10 years.

From Joshua: Thank you to my wife, Courtney, for your willingness to join me in making this project a reality and for your steadfast encouragement to follow the call of our God.

To our Board of Directors, donors and ministry partners, thank you for your continued support and encouragement of the Kingdom work that is taking place around the world. Without you, there would be no words to fill the pages of this book.

Most importantly, thank you to the one, true, living God that called us all to take the message of the gospel to the ends of the earth and who provided a way for us to do that through Doulos and our partners.

Doulos Partners
2018 Leadership

Board of Directors

Thomas Minor, Chairman
Lev Bragg, Vice Chairman Partner Relations
Mark Fillers, Vice Chairman Development
Kevin Halcomb, Vice Chairman Administration
David Johnson, Founder & CEO
Scott Gurosky, Founder
Wayne Myrick, Founder

Rick Burgess	Rusty Hicks	Glenn Parker
Jim Croft	Tofey Leon	Ben Short
Rusty Favorite	Gregg Morrison	Gary York

Junior Board

Caleb Bagwell	Jenn Bragg
Patrick Dreher	Will Johnston
Mason Phillips	

Staff

David Johnson	Founder & CEO
Josh Clarke	President
Susan Johnson	Office Manager
Marcia Lowry	Administrative Assistant
Brian Johnson	IT Coordinator

Contents

FOREWORD
By Rick Burgess

Co-Host of the Nationally Syndicated
Rick and Bubba Show

"All authority in heaven and on earth has been given to me. Go therefore and make disciples of all nations, baptizing them in the name of the Father and of the Son and of the Holy Spirit, teaching them to obey all that I have commanded you. And behold, I am with you always, even to the end of the age." Matthew 28:18-20

When I was honored with the request to write the foreword for this book about Doulos Partners, this passage of Scripture was the first thing that came to my mind.

I certainly will not thill any reader with my certificates from a world-renown seminary. However, I am not sure one is needed to place the importance on these words given to us by Jesus Christ. The most glaring evidence lies in the fact that this is one of the last things Jesus said to His followers before ascending to heaven. Can you imagine how close you would listen if you had been there?

Jesus had been teaching for three years. He had been to the cross and paid the price for all sin- past, present and future. He had defeated eternal death by walking out of the tomb on the third day. He continued to teach for forty more days. Then right before He left this earth, He declared that He had one more thing He wanted us to know. He delivered these commandments found in Matthew 28:18-20.
Hey...that's a really big deal!

I remember the first time I heard the word *doulos*, Scott Gurosky was telling me about a ministry called Doulos Partners. This Greek word means a bond servant, one who has given up their own rights to be completely under the authority of Christ and to His service. The Apostle Paul said he was "doulos" to Christ.

I loved the name and thought it was perfect for the call that God had placed on this ministry. Scott and I had become friends while he helped me on the journey to see all that God was and is still doing after tragedy struck and my wife and I buried our two-year-old son, Bronner. Sherrie and I put together a memorial fund in his name to be used to advance the Kingdom of God.

We decided that every grant we would approve could only go to ministries that were evangelical and following the final instructions of Jesus Christ. Scott began to show me the vision of Doulos Partners and it didn't take very long to decide that we would use a portion of the money in Bronner's memorial fund to help Doulos Partners carry out its mission.

As believers, we are to tell people the good news of what God did through His Son to reconcile all mankind to a holy God, and to make disciples and to teach them to obey His commands.

Now we have come to a looming question. What is to be the plan for carrying out this enormous mandate? I am not the first person to point out that these clear instructions from Christ have many times been called the "Great Omission" from the "Great Commission." Why? Because it's difficult and requires time and money to properly equip an American to leave his or her country to go to a foreign land, learn the language, learn the culture, be accepted by the culture, etc.

What we find is that so much time and money is spent earning the right to share the gospel and disciple the new believers that it just isn't that effective.

Let me be clear, my family and I go on short term mission trips, and of course, there are many missionaries from our country and around the world that are answering the call they are certain came from God. I am not suggesting that there is no place for this type of mission work. However, the plan laid out by Doulos Partners is incredibly effective. Going all over the world and finding followers of Christ who need training, money and accountability to reach and disciple their own people just *works*. The return on our investment in this plan of equipping the indigenous people to reach and disciple their own nation far exceeds any other plan that I have personally seen.

The accountability was another thing that drew us to Doulos Partners. I was able to get a very clear picture of this when I was honored to be asked to serve as a board member for Doulos Partners. The theology, the curriculum and the church plants are all highly vetted.

My wife and I continue to be blown away by how God is producing so much fruit around the world through this simple but effective strategy to make disciples as instructed by Jesus Christ. I hope you will prayerfully consider joining us on this commission to "go therefore and make disciples of all nations." The commands from Jesus Christ are quite clear and only the things we invest in the Kingdom of God will stand in eternity.

SECTION 1

2:32 A.M. – The Beginning

PROLOGUE

I have a love-hate relationship with a digital clock. When I wake up in the middle of the night and wonder what time it is, I love to look at a digital clock. Maybe it's the peace of mind it gives to know that I haven't overslept or that I am right on time. There are occasions, though, when I am restless. It is those nights that I watch the display change minute by minute, with sleep nowhere in sight.

I will never forget the digital clock on that night in late October of 2007, when the Lord woke me up out of a deep sleep. I went from sound asleep to wide awake in mere seconds. My faculties were firing on all cylinders and my mind was sharp, as if I had been awake for hours. I looked at the clock and it was 2:32 AM. God woke me up, came in quickly and downloaded.

For those of us who have journeyed with the Lord, we know His voice when He speaks to us. I knew without a doubt this was from Him. In the past, He had given a word to me or prompted me to action, but this was different. It felt different. My body responded differently. It was a new direction, a new course, for the next piece of the journey that He had set out for me.

This is what I heard: "I have a new assignment for you. I am going to move you from micro to macro ministry. I want you in every country on every inhabitabed continent. Give. Go. Ask. Expect." And just like that, I was left to ponder what in the world all that meant.

CHAPTER 1
What's in a Name?

Let me back up a little to help you understand the context of my encounter.

There are those moments in life when you are studying the Scripture and all of a sudden you come across a word that jumps off the page. It is almost as if it comes alive to you in that moment. It changes your day, your month, your life. It changes your forever.

That very thing happened to me in September of 2007 as I was studying to preach through the book of Philippians as the pastor of Dayspring Baptist Church in Mobile, Alabama. I was preparing that week for the introductory message to a new sermon series. I could have never imagined what the Lord was going to do with the trajectory of my life as I began to read. Philippians 1:1 (NKJV) says, *"Paul and Timothy,* **bondservants** *of Christ Jesus, to all the saints in Christ Jesus who are in Philippi, with the bishops and deacons."*

When I saw the word "bondservants" on the page, it was as if it was bolded. I knew it wasn't literally that way in my Bible, but it seemed to jump off the page at me. My attention was drawn completely to that word and the meaning it held for Paul as he wrote it to the members of the church at Philippi.

It had become a habit of mine during my personal study and sermon preparation to see words and try to recall them in the original Greek. This time, though, it did not matter how hard I tried, I could not remember the original meaning for the word "bondservant." The Greek language is rich and, often times, there are deeper meanings that get lost as the word is translated into English. As I opened up my concordances and began a study on this word "bondservant," I realized that the deepest, truest meaning had been lost in translation.

The word used by Paul here is the word "doulos."

There were three different English translations of this word that would appear throughout the New Testament 141 times. While many translate it as "servant" or "bondservant," the most accurate meaning in the Greek is the word "slave." I understand the emotion you just experienced as you read that word. Knowing the sinful history of our country with the slave trade, my body almost recoiled as I read it aloud. However, I had to remind myself that the word used here by Paul was not talking about human slavery. It was talking about spiritual slavery.

For the next thirty days, every waking moment, I continued to face the word "doulos." No matter where I was or what I was doing, I was confronted with the thought that I am called to be a slave to the Lord.

I would reread that first verse in Philippians many times. Paul gave himself the title of a slave of Jesus Christ. He is not doing so in a moment of weakness or sadness but rather, he is wearing it as a badge of honor with great joy. What would it mean to truly be found faithful as a slave to Christ?

My mind raced to Matthew chapter six, where Jesus tells us that we cannot serve two masters. We would hate the one and love the other or be devoted to one and despise the other. This is a stark reminder from Jesus that our heart was not made to split its allegiances, but it can only surrender to and serve one master. I continued to wrestle with this idea that you cannot serve both God and anything else. We would choose to serve God or we would choose to serve an idol that we placed before Him.

This train of thought and what it meant for my life and ministry was all-consuming. I pondered what the master-slave relationship would look like with the Lord. More than anything, it was the battle of trying to piece together my revulsion to the word slavery while fully understanding that scripture calls us to be a slave to God.

As I continued to move through this time, all I could think of was what God expected of me as His follower. I struggled with the meaning of this relationship of a master and a slave. The more I studied, the more I began to put aside my American view of the word slave and pick up the biblical meaning. I began to see that it wasn't a coerced or legalistic view of following God, but rather a yearning to follow Him in every way. The paradox: I was both shackled and free. My relationship with Him enhances my walk with Him. The one thing that he expects from me and from you as His followers is boiled down to one word: obedience. My love for him is shown by my desire and willingness to lay aside *me* and to fully follow His commands.

I felt like the Lord had taken me on this journey in order to fully understand the series I was to preach and, as I soon realized, it would play a more personal role than I could have ever imagined. I would need to be fully committed to God, trusting in His place and promise for my life.

So when He woke me up in October of 2007, the seed of Doulos Partners had already been planted and was taking root so that my *yes* would be fully on the table.

> The one thing He expects from me and from you as His followers is boiled down to one word: obedience.

CHAPTER 2
A Cord of Three Strands

The founding of Doulos Partners happened from different parts of the state of Alabama, as well as from three different people. The Lord worked simultaneously in the hearts of Scott Gurosky, Wayne Myrick, and myself. He began to prepare us for a life-changing call even before we knew what the assignment was that He had for us to accomplish.

In the following pages, Scott, Wayne, and I will give you a look at the journeys that the Lord used with each of us to begin the work called Doulos Partners. It truly is a wonderful example of how the Lord speaks to His people for His purpose and how "a threefold cord is not easily broken."

Scott's Story

• • •

In my almost fifty years on this earth, I have only been a member of two churches and have only been pastored by four men and I think that's remarkable. The church I was raised in and joined as a believer was Pleasant Ridge Baptist Church in Hueytown, Alabama. The church I joined as a teenager and spent the next thirty-four years attending is Shades Mountain Baptist Church in Vestavia Hills, Alabama.

The four men that served as my pastors in the course of those years were Reverend Judson Jones, Dr. Billy Harris, Dr. Charles Carter and Dr. Danny Wood. These four men, along with their congregations, were very instrumental in my growth and maturity as a follower of Christ and I owe them all a huge "thank you" for their investment in my life. My part of the Doulos story would not have occurred without God using all of these people at the times He did to help guide and teach me as an ever-maturing Christian.

Growing up in Hueytown, Alabama, was an unbelievable blessing to me. By modern standards, it was a small town and our church family at Pleasant Ridge was truly that- a family. My parents, Mike and Linda Gurosky, were very involved in all aspects of our church and there was never a time in my childhood that my entire family was not involved. Even neighborhood and social activities were spent with the same friends from our church family.

Being part of this true community of believers was a special and extremely impactful time in my life. A time that I wouldn't fully recognize or appreciate until we took our first mission trip with Doulos to Cuba in 2008.

In 1983, my family moved from Hueytown to Vestavia Hills, where we joined Shades Mountain Baptist Church. I was a freshman in high school and truthfully, as a student, I drifted away from church life.

It was only after I was married that my wife, Kelly and I started putting effort towards being a part of the church. We joined a "young marrieds" class that was taught by Lev and Vicki Bragg. Kelly and I were drawn to Lev and Vicki's teaching and leadership and God used them in a profound way to influence our lives, not only as spiritual role models, but also as trusted mentors and friends. Ultimately, Lev would be instrumental in helping me maneuver through the calling that God would place on my heart in helping to start Doulos Partners.

The moral of the story is that our impact, our lives and our witness are important and help shape, in one way or another, those in whom we invest. I'm so thankful to those who invested in my family and me.

Fast forward to 2002. Danny Wood, our pastor at Shades Mountain Baptist, was being led to start an annual Global Impact Celebration (GIC). During this week-long event, we would invite missionaries from around the world to come to our church, where we would celebrate their work in advancing the gospel. It was like nothing I had ever been involved with, and it instantly put "missions" on the forefront of my mind.

Interestingly, like so many, I had been in church my

entire life, but had never given missions any serious thought regarding my personal involvement. As the GIC grew each year, it became one of the true identifiers of Shades Mountain Baptist and its continued success has become a model for churches around the country today.

By 2007, Kelly and I had two wonderful sons: Davis (10 yrs. old) and Drew (7 yrs. old). Davis had given his life to Christ a year or so earlier, and Drew would do the same within a couple of years, so God was working in a powerful way within our family. I think it was during the 2007 GIC when, completely out of the blue, Davis leaned over to me during the service and whispered, "When are you going to take us on a mission trip?"

My heart sank. I instantly felt like the biggest failure as a dad, husband and "Christian" on earth! I immediately responded with something to the effect of "Right away!" Little did I know that God was using Davis, and his obedience as a child, to wake me up to what He wanted me to do. That one question from Davis literally set into motion a life-changing series of events.

The next day, I called the church and asked for a list of every mission trip that was scheduled. When I received it, there was nothing that grabbed my attention, nothing to which I was drawn.

I in no way felt that the trips scheduled through the church were not needed or of lesser value because of my lack of connection, because that's not the case. Looking back, I believe it simply highlighted the fact that God had other plans for me. May we never be so arrogant to think that we have it "figured out" and that others can't be used in ways to which we aren't drawn. It was just not my calling to be a part of the trips that our church had planned that year.

I was being drawn to something bigger than a mission trip, or even a series of mission trips. I was being lead to look at missions in a much different way than I had ever heard or seen before, and though I wasn't sure what it would ultimately look like, I was sure that God was the catalyst behind what I was experiencing.

> **May we never be so arrogant to think that we have it "figured out" and that others can't be used in ways to which we aren't drawn.**

The men that have had the most impact on my life - my father (Mike Gurosky), my high school baseball coach (Sammy Dunn), and my business partner (Wayne Myrick) all shared and lived out specific values and character traits that I've tried to embrace in my life:

1.) A high value on giving tremendous effort in whatever you're doing.
2.) Simplifying life and goals, so as to not get bogged down in things that can prevent you from from being successful.
3.) Placing a high value on results (winning).

In 2007, my application of these values led me to the belief that missions as a whole lacked most, if not all of these traits.

Now before you get upset about that statement, you should take a real assessment of what has and has not been accomplished over the past 2,000 years. I am *not* saying that all missionaries aren't working hard, nor am I saying that all mission's initiatives aren't focused on results, but I am saying that a non-emotional and logical evaluation of the big picture of Christian Missions, in my opinion, yields facts that speak to the contrary of us (Christians, the church, etc.) being very successful in what Christ has called us to do.

My logic was/is simple (at least, to me). Think about it. As of 2018, the estimated population of earth stands at approximately 7.5 billion. Of those 7.5 billion, it's estimated that almost 4.5 billion have indeed heard the name of Jesus, which is roughly the same number of people who currently have access to the Internet around the world. So, in less than thirty years (the World Wide Web was invented in 1989) we have been able to get internet access to the same number of people that it has taken us around 2,000 years to tell about Jesus.

This statistic, in my mind, makes a strong argument against the historical effectiveness and approach to missions. Maybe you feel like that analogy is over simplified, or possibly you fall into the trap of thinking it's a "resourcing" problem.

Here is some additional food for thought.

It's believed that Christians invest upwards of $30 billion per year on "missions" and an additional $500 billion on other "Christian causes." Even using greatly reduced figures we can safely assume that, in just the past twenty-five years alone, Christians have invested between

$5-$7 trillion in missions and Christian causes—and we still have over 3 billion people that have never heard of Jesus?

I personally believe this understanding quickly leads to the conclusion that, on a macro scale, our approach to missions has not worked.

It's the above perspective that God used in my life to plant the seed of developing a missions organization that would paint outside the lines of modern day evangelism logic. The focus, in my mind, needed to be placed on simplicity, efficiency and effectiveness—the same three traits that had been ingrained in me my entire life by those God had placed around me.

I've always told my kids that there is a very fine line between being a leader and a loner, and to determine which you are, you simply have to look behind you. If no one is following, then you're a loner! God would have to find and introduce me to people with the same heart as mine or I was simply going to be a one man want-to-be (a loner). God gave me a very clear directive: "See this through." I understood what that meant because I often had good ideas, but after a few tough months and several, "We're not interested(s)", I would get discouraged and just move on. That attitude was not going to work, so God faithfully hammered me daily on "seeing it through" — whatever "it" was.

My first visit was with Lev Bragg, my "young married" Sunday School teacher I spoke of earlier, who had become a dear friend and a man whose opinion I really valued. He was also a man that I knew to be a "hard sell," so I thought if I could convince him on what I was thinking, then I'd be set.

We met at a local restaurant and I began telling him about this "great idea" that I had for a mission's organization and let's just say that he seemed less than impressed.

He certainly wasn't ready to start writing checks or get a "Doulos" tattoo, but he did give me what I believe now was God-ordained advice: "Don't think you have to do something different than everyone else, just find someone who's already doing it well and join them."

He wasn't quoting *Experiencing God*, he was being honest in his view of where he had seen similar ideas fall apart. I didn't like his advice because it took me, my creativity, and my initiatives, and put them in the hands of others. After all, wasn't this really supposed to be about me? Not hardly and I would quickly learn that there were some real heavy-weights deep into the fight that just needed support.

My next visit was to Wayne Myrick, my business partner of thirteen years at the time and a man I trusted and relied on. I quickly realized that God was obviously working in his life in a similar way that He was working in mine. Knowing Wayne was behind it meant I didn't need to worry about not seeing it through—that's never been an option for Wayne.

Once Wayne commits, I've known few people who can see things through more thoroughly or effectively than him.

Interestingly, several years earlier, Wayne and I— through our company Myrick, Gurosky & Associates—had started a private foundation to help those in physical need that were unable to help themselves. We used proceeds from our company to fund the efforts and only the executives in our company and a couple of others knew about it.

It was not something that we wanted publicized because we know how people can turn good into bad. We needed a name for the foundation, so we asked an employee who helped in our Business Development area at the time to come up with a name. After some time, he came back to Wayne and I with the name "Doulos." My first reaction was that he was over thinking it; however, one idea behind the organization was to ensure that we (MG&A) were kept at arms-length, and anyone who knew Wayne or I would quickly think we weren't clever enough to come up with that name, so we went with it.

Our company was able to do some great work through the Doulos Foundation. The state of Alabama (specifically the Birmingham area) endured a period of years where we experienced devastating tornadoes and through God's grace on our business, we were able to help quite a few people with their needs.

Eventually, we shared with the rest of MG&A's employees that the Doulos Foundation existed, and its purpose and they started bringing in requests for those they knew that were in need. It was a very special time in the history of our company. We were able to help those around us through the efforts of some of our employees, who thought enough of those in need to bring them to our attention.

Given that we already had a foundation (named after a Greek word pulled directly from Scripture) we felt the name Doulos would have great possibility as we prayed about starting a missions organization. We now had a direction and a name, but we still didn't have any international missions relationships or anyone to lead the ministry. As I prayed about it, God put a man named Manny Fernandez on my mind and heart. Manny was a keynote speaker at one of the GIC celebrations at Shades Mountain Baptist Church. Amazingly, of all the great speakers I had heard over the years at our GICs, Manny was the only person whose name I remembered. He was one of the most compelling speakers that I had ever heard (and still is). Though we had never met, I felt strongly that God was telling me to call him, so I did. That phone conversation led us to a potential partnership and a trip that we would be taking with Manny in February of 2008.

We had a directive, a name, a possible partner and a mission trip planned, but we still didn't have a clear idea of the role in missions that Doulos would play. Having a potential partnership with World Link was fantastic, but it didn't constitute us being a "ministry" and we still didn't have a leader.

But, God was way ahead of us.

David Johnson was a man I met through Wayne while David served as Executive Pastor at Hunter Street Baptist in Birmingham. We have had the privilege of working with some of the best Executive Pastors in the country, but I'd never seen anyone more effective at that position than David. Through our years of working with Hunter Street, he and I became good friends.

David left Hunter Street in 2001 to become the Senior Pastor at Dayspring Baptist Church in Mobile, Alabama, and our relationship continued to grow as we became the Design-Builder for multiple projects at Dayspring.

In November of 2007, not long after talking with Manny, David contacted us and asked if he could come see Wayne and me. We assumed that it was to discuss another project at Dayspring and though we were excited about that, we both talked about how we thought David would be the perfect person to run Doulos— though I don't think either of us thought it was a real possibility.

David came to see us and got right to the point. He said that God had really been working in his life and had woken him up on a number of occasions, telling him that he needed to go see three people and Wayne and I were two of the three.

God had also given David a word that he was confident that Wayne and I had never heard of: *Doulos.*

We let him ramble on about the definition, where it was used in Scripture, etc. as if we were really learning something.

After about fifteen minutes of *Doulos* explanations, I said, "We've had a foundation named Doulos for almost ten years now, and we understand what it means and how the word is used in Scripture."

The look on David's face was priceless. He just stared at Wayne and me, and then he said, "Why didn't you tell me you had this organization called Doulos?"

I responded, "Because it was none of your business."

We went on to explain why we had kept it a secret and we all got a good laugh out of the moment, but it was crystal clear to all of us that God had ordained that meeting and that time.

Wayne's Story

• • •

As I write this section, I am sixty-seven years old. I am thankful for the opportunity to look back and think about all that has happened - and, to my surprise, I am still breathing!

I never thought I would live past sixty years of age. My dad died of a heart attack at the age of fifty-four while I was still very young. I really didn't know what was happening then, but I knew things changed fast after that, and not much of it was good. Let's just say I became independent very young in life.

When I was nine, for some reason that I don't recall, I was attending a revival at Oak Grove Baptist Church. I remember it like it was yesterday. That is saying a lot since I don't remember very much else now a-days. The Pastor was talking about sin and salvation and it all made sense. I knew God's call on me was to trust him. Unfortunately, that trust could only go as far as what I knew, and it wasn't very much. So, I, like many people, strayed for the next twenty years. My exposure to godly influences were few and far between.

The next time I encountered God, it was through brokenness from my own independence. God would use that to let me know He had never left me and I heard Him calling me back to Himself.

During that time of renewal, I developed a habit of reading the book of Proverbs every day. The first verse that I became connected to in a special way was Proverbs

4:23: *"Keep your heart with all vigilance, for from it flow the springs of life."* I believe that single verse opened up the entire Bible to me. At twenty-eight, I began to not just read God's Word, but to think about God's Word which would later develop into a passion for God's Word. It has never stopped speaking to me since then. I cannot say I have always listened, but it has been quick to provide direction.

I have been a member of three churches in my life: Oak Grove Baptist, Pleasant Ridge Baptist and Hunter Street Baptist, which I have now been a member of for more than three decades. Our family was one of the first to join Hunter Street after they had relocated from the western side of Birmingham to Hoover, Alabama. I am so thankful that God lead us to that church and to our pastor Buddy Gray, as well as Topper Reid and David Johnson. These brothers have had a profound impact on my life along with the many friends we have made there over the years.

Had we not found Hunter Street Baptist Church, I am not sure I would be as close to God as I am today (which, by the way, is still much too far away). Our church home has been a constant source of growth and encouragement to my wife, Lynn, and me. Through our time there, I believe we have been able to really find God. This brings me to the next verse from Proverbs that came to have real meaning

Seeking diligently is time-consuming hard work, but the benefit is living in God's presence in a real way.

to me and a verse that I often reflect on. Proverbs 8:17: *"I love those who love me, and those who seek me diligently find me."* Seeking diligently is time-consuming hard work, but the benefit is living in God's presence in a real way.

God was doing much to prepare Lynn and me for what was to become Doulos Partners. In the beginning years at Hunter Street we were very active in the church in a traditional way. I led several mission trips with large groups of people to remodel and renovate churches in the United States, and I had also led several trips to Brazil to build church buildings. At the same time, we were in the beginnings of our company, Myrick, Gurosky & Associates, which specializes in church development, design and construction. With fifty years of construction experience, thirty-two of which were spent dedicated to the building of church facilities, I have seen the good, the bad, and the ugly of church life.

Southern Baptist churches are encouraged to give some percentage of the annual budget to the Cooperative Program to fund missions. Pastors tend to be judged by their peers on how much the church gives and, in denominational life, this may come into play for being elected to some leadership position. There is seemingly no accountability related to the giving. Usually, at some point during the year, the missionaries will come back to their respective states and tour the local churches talking about their particular missionary assignment. When I would review the impact that these missionaries were having it seemed rather small. I would hear stories of missionaries that spent their whole lives on the mission field with very little success, as if that were a reason to keep on with the same strategies.

I am not saying that I think all SBC missionaries are ineffective. I am sure that many serve well. But it would seem the plan of sending Americans into countries we have been going to for decades to reach a people and culture that is foreign to them is questionable as a primary strategy.

Topper Reid came to Hunter Street Baptist Church as the Education Minister. Topper was very entrepreneurial when it came to getting the congregation involved in new things. He asked if I would lead a mission trip to Maine to do some renovations to a church in a small town.

I was excited to be involved, so Topper and I made a trip to the church to find out what needed to be done. We solicited a team of about forty people and that summer, we set out to do the work.

Of course, this included a stopover in New York City for sightseeing by the majority of our people.

We made a significant difference in the appearance of the church, but I don't recall anyone spreading the Gospel. The next year we did the same thing in New Jersey and again I came away wondering, "What was the point?" I did get to know some of my fellow "Hunter Streeters" better, and maybe that was the point.

After that, I took a few years off until Buddy ask me to lead a group to Brazil to build six churches. We did that for two years. I can tell you some good stories and we got to know even more people at Hunter Street. But was that the point of the trip? Maybe so!

I became very frustrated with the church's idea of missions. I also became very frustrated with my own lack of effectiveness in this area.

So, I stopped being led to do what someone else thought was a good idea for a mission project. But I didn't stop seeking God. In fact, I think in many ways, it fueled the fire to seek Him more. I was seeing that the traditional way wasn't working. I didn't see any change in people's lives as a result of these mission efforts or my own. I think I may have been seeking man's approval, not God's.

I became more curious than ever about what God's word had to say about how we serve him during our brief time in this fallen world. The more I learned about who God is, the more I learned about my own failings.

For the next ten years, I spent more time studying God's word and trying to apply it. The typical church member's life didn't seem to me to mirror what I was reading in Scripture and that included me.
I read a book by Charles Colson and Nancy Pearcey, called *How Now Shall We Live?*

The title drew me in because it reflected what I was searching for. The book was very challenging to read, but it solidified my quest for personal holiness. The closer I got to God's presence, the further away I seemed to be so I continued to seek God more. It's a non-human kind of response, isn't it?

One day, I saw Buddy in the parking lot, and I mentioned to him I had read the book by Colson. He looked at me like a dog looking at a TV. After the initial shock, he said he was starting a theological reading group, and he asked if I wanted to join. I don't think I would have been asked if we hadn't met in the parking lot and had the discussion. I don't think he thought of me in that way.

Certainly, I was the slowest horse in the race as our group met. My journey began by doing weekly reading groups with minimal lapses from one group to the next.

I am thankful for that encounter with Buddy that morning because seeking God became a natural pursuit rather than another church activity.

Over the next fifteen years, as I searched and read, I came upon another verse that has stuck with me. It was a summation of Scripture that I can rely on to fulfill all of God's message. Romans 5:8: *"But God shows his love for us in that while we were still sinners, Christ died for us."*

Now the question is, what do we do with that other than make another set of rules to live by that satisfy the letter of the law but not the intent? As Jesus said in the Sermon on the Mount "You have heard it said... but I tell you...", the first thing Jesus needed to do was to reprogram the thinking of his followers by teaching what a Christian is.

Dr. Martyn Lloyd Jones's book, *Studies in the Sermon on the Mount* carries a continuous theme throughout that "a Christian is before a Christian does". This is completely backwards to the typical church experience.

Church is a great place to be on Sunday—my favorite place to be, in fact. But at some point, we have to ask: Is that good enough? Is that what Jesus was trying to teach in Matthew 5?

Church does a great job of providing structure for believers in practical ways: a place to gather, people to gather with, a way to worship, and all of it wrapped up in a neat package. Expectation given and expectation met. Not a lot to consider, just show up.

I am not saying that the pastors of churches intended it to be that way; it is just the way most of them end up. The easiest thing for me would have been to keep leading mission trips and building things, but that felt really wrong, really inadequate, really self-serving.

So, in 2007, David Johnson showed up with a question about the same things I was asking myself. God was certainly calling me to consider something different. It would be both challenging and satisfying. God knew before time that this day would come and that He had prepared David, Scott, and me for the same question, one that many people throughout history have asked: Is there a better way?

We found that, just like those who have gone before us, all who seek Him in truth, they will find Him and His loving kindness.

God had prepared Scott and me for this time in our business as well. We had experienced a five-year stretch of growth and maturity as a company. We had a good core group that are still with us today.

Had we known what was coming in the next seven years, however, it may have all been different. I would hope not, but who knows? The decision was an easy one in 2008, but the decision to complete the job was much harder.

We all know what happened in our economy from 2009 to 2016, but I don't think most people really knew the impact. Our company went from having a tremendous backlog of work to almost no work. Our staffing was radically reduced as we finished up jobs. The employees that remained had their pay reduced significantly. We were forced to put money into the company that would clean out our personal accounts. We sold our office building that I loved and used the equity to sustain the company. To put it simply, we were tapped out! So making good on our three-year commitment to pay David's salary in full and to provide the seed money to start Doulos Partners was both physically and spiritually challenging. However, the next eight years ended up being the best years of my life.

David's Story

• • •

In my quiet time in the middle of November 2007, the Lord spoke to me again and gave me the names of three men; John Wright, Wayne Myrick and Scott Gurosky. They were all longtime friends. The Lord impressed upon me that I was supposed to travel to Birmingham and share with them about what He had said to me that early morning in late October.

I called them, made appointments, took a vacation day, and traveled to Birmingham to have a conversation about a calling I hadn't fully fleshed out.

The first appointment was with John, a friend for over twenty years. I will never forget that meeting as we sat down at lunch for some barbeque. At this point, there were only two other people on the planet who knew what the Lord had done in my life. John was about to be the third. As we faced each other across the table, I tried my best to explain what little I knew about what God was asking me to do. We talked about the four words, His call to a more global focus on ministry, and the way God had led me to the word *doulos*.

As I concluded, John looked up and he said "When you get it figured out, call me. I'm in!"

With my limited understanding of what the Lord had for me to do, I was somewhat surprised at John's willingness to commit to join in something that was not yet a reality. He understood that the calling was still unfolding, but he knew that God was going to provide clarity and wanted him to be involved. This proved to not be an empty promise. Since that meeting until today, John has continued to walk alongside Doulos with his love, his prayers and his financial support.

Leaving John, I proceeded to the next meeting with Wayne Myrick and Scott Gurosky. Not only were these two men dear friends, but we had done a lot of business together. Myrick, Gurosky and Associates, Inc. is a premier design/build company for churches nationwide. The three of us had worked on many projects together at Hunter Street Baptist Church and Dayspring Baptist Church. Probably, in their minds, this was going to be another similar meeting to lay out a plan for the next phase of construction. They were no doubt surprised at what the Lord was stirring within me and what I had to say.

As I explained the word doulos and the importance of the call to macro ministry, Wayne and Scott kept giving each other weird looks. It was as if they knew something that was happening that I didn't. Scott then turned to me and asked if I was aware that already in existence within their company was the Doulos Foundation. It was in that moment with those two men that the Holy Spirit moved and confirmed the call that the Lord had placed on my life.

It was one of those flashes where God seemed to be saying, "Don't miss what's happening here."

You see, even after all of my work with these men and their company over a thirteen-year period, I had never heard of the Doulos Foundation. It was truly a providential moment. This foundation was set up to take some of the profits of MG&A and to help those in need without drawing attention to the company itself. By taking the company's name out of the foundation, it allowed them to focus on giving the glory to the Lord. I had never heard of it because I was never meant to hear of it. But the name Doulos assured us that it was more than a coincidence.

After the meeting, Scott pulled me aside to tell me what the Lord was doing in his life regarding the Great Commission. Earlier that year, he had been at his home church and the Lord clearly called him and his family to be an active part of the Kingdom work that was taking place in Cuba. They were planning a trip to the island in February of 2008 and he invited me to join him to see what God was doing. Without even a moment of hesitation, I accepted. It was evident through our time together that God was up to something and I did not want to be even one step behind.

I left Birmingham after having those two meetings with a great sense of excitement about what God was doing. We still were not sure exactly what it was, how it was going to look or what it all meant, but our *yes* was on the table.

In the middle of December, I received a phone call from Scott. He had a word from the Lord about the next steps to take. As I listened, he proceeded to tell me that he felt that the Lord had

> **We still were not sure exactly what it was, how it was going to look or what it all meant, but our *yes* was on the table.**

ordained this moment in time and that I was supposed to be the leader of whatever was being formed. While humbled, I reminded Scott that there wasn't anything to be in charge of. There was no clear direction of what we were supposed to do or who we were as an organization. Full of confidence in what God was saying to him, Scott acknowledged those things to be true while still looking forward to what God was seemingly doing in our midst.

December and January are always busy in church life and this was no exception. As I juggled my role as pastor, the Lord continued to prepare my heart for the trip to Cuba in February. Meanwhile, being men of action, Scott and Wayne began moving forward with the process of creating a legal entity for the ministry.

The only thing that existed at this point was a private foundation, not a non-profit (among other regulations, a private foundation is restricted to a $300,000.00 limit on funds received).

We decided on the name "Doulos Ministries" and Paul Head, CFO of MG&A, filed the Articles of Incorporation through a local law firm in Birmingham, Alabama to start the process in January 2008. So, with the necessary legal documents under way, it was time to go to Cuba and see what the Lord was doing and what He was going to show us about the next steps in our journey.

I got on a plane in the middle of February to travel to Cuba, still without a clear understanding of what purpose the Lord had for me in this plan but knowing that I was right in the middle of His will.

As I got off the plane in Havana, I met Manny Fernandez and Felix Diez, who were leading the work there. While exchanging greetings and introductions, I could feel the power of the Holy Spirit and had an instant connection with these brothers. After only about ten minutes of being on the ground, I knew that this was what God was calling me to do. It was an unmistakable moment of clarity and affirmation.

So clear, in fact, that immediately upon returning from the trip, I called the Personnel Committee of Dayspring Baptist Church and resigned from the role of pastor.

In the days following, we laid out a plan that would ensure a seamless transition for the church that wouldn't hinder the work that God was doing there but would allow me to walk forward in the new assignment He had for me. Scott and Wayne committed to provide the financial support, including my salary, for the first three years of the ministry's existence. All three of us officially put our yes on the table, not only in word but in action, trusting that the Lord would continue to show us His way.

We unanimously agreed that we were going to function as a partnering organization and needed to amend the name from Doulos Ministries to Doulos Partners. After the name change and the completion of our Articles of Incorporation, Paul filed the 1023, which is the request to the IRS to become a recognized 501(c)(3) organization, in late February of 2008.

March 30, 2008 was my last day at Dayspring Baptist Church and on April 1, I drove to Birmingham to begin the work. I walked into my office that day (provided by MG&A), and those first few moments are still fresh on my mind. I looked around to see a clear desk and an empty filing cabinet. There was much work to be done for the

Kingdom.

Those first weeks, we spent a lot of time talking over how exactly we were supposed to complete the task that the Lord had given us, to take the gospel to the ends of the earth. There was a great need for resources, both financial and spiritual, but God was already raising up the workers in His harvest field. He was showing us that we could be more effective in His call and His work by partnering with indigenous leaders who have a passion to reach their own countrymen for Christ. This understanding and clarity provided the path for the work that was set before us.

On April 11, 2008, we received our 501(c)(3) paperwork from the IRS and Doulos Partners was officially born. There were no other donors, no completed partnerships, and no work being done in the field that was officially ours. There was, however, a clear call from the Lord and willing hearts saying yes to that call even though we did not fully understand all that He had in store for us in the years ahead. An incredible beginning to what was to become a God-sized story!

CHAPTER 3
The Importance of the Indigenous

Growing up, I was very fortunate. I was brought up in a Christian home where I was taken to church by my mom and dad, Wayne and Yvonne Johnson. Vacation Bible School for me was cookies and Kool Aid and playing kickball outside. I do, however remember the lessons about missionaries.

As I got older, Wednesday nights were all about Royal Ambassadors and learning even more about missions around the world. Occasionally, our church would have a missionary come and speak at a service. They would talk about what the Lord was doing with their ministry and what life was like on the field. The stories fascinated me and I was moved by their decision to live in a foreign place. They had to learn a different language and transplant their families into a different culture. It was the greatest level of sacrifice and commitment that I had ever seen.

Looking back on that time, I realize I had a very limited understanding of missions. The English Oxford Dictionary defines a missionary as "a person sent on a religious mission, especially one sent to promote Christianity in a foreign country." Because of my church background, this was my definition of a missionary well into adulthood. It wasn't until much later in my life that the Lord would broaden my view.

First as an Executive Pastor and then as a Senior Pastor, I watched how missions dollars were spent. I understood the costs associated with having a western missionary on the field and the high burnout rate within this group. I began to wonder if there were other ways of accomplishing the Great Commission.

God began to stir inside of me a desire to discover a different missions strategy to evangelize the world. He showed me that westerners are now some of the least trusted in our global society and that there are also closed countries where missionaries of any country are not welcomed to share the gospel. The Middle East, Africa, and Central and Southeast Asia are seeing a rapidly growing reality of martyrdom. My mind constantly echoed, "There must be a more expedient and efficient way."

I finally saw a perfect picture of this on my first trip to Cuba. I observed first-hand the passion of indigenous pastors who desired to see their own people reached for Christ and churches planted in their own neighborhoods. Even more than the logistical and economic benefits, the love that these indigenous leaders had for their own countrymen provided a strong foundation for their long-term success.

Regardless of what country I find myself in, there is a deep and abiding love within the indigenous leader for their neighbors, friends and family members. There is a passion and desire within them to see their country won for Christ that is unlike anything I have seen or experienced before. They work tirelessly with such efficiency.

It was the closest thing I had ever seen to the first century church. Their methods were cost effective and simplistic. It made such practical sense. They were insiders and didn't have the problem of cultural or language barriers. After all, they were speaking their native tongue in the culture of their birth. They didn't have to learn to navigate laws and government restrictions. They were Nationals, not hindered by outside affluence or distractions. These pastors were biblical literalists: they read it, they believed it and they practiced it.

This experience inspired my current understanding that indigenous leaders are, for lack of a better phrase, set up for success. They have full access to countries where foreigners may face difficulties obtaining a long-term visa. They are able to live and work within the country because they are citizens. They know the country, they know the culture, they know the people. They are able to understand the lies Satan uses against the people, because at one point in time, they believed them as well. They are able to speak to the heart of cultural apprehensions because it is their culture and heritage. They are quickly able to build trust and relationships because they are one of their own. Most of the time, people implicitly trust other people who are like them.

Taking those difficulties of western missionaries into consideration, Doulos Partners began to see the opportunity to work alongside and empower indigenous believers to take the gospel to their own countries. Since our inception, we have seen this strategy have a high success rate in both countries that are open to the sharing of the gospel as well as those who have strict laws forbidding it.

There is also an economic advantage to empowering indigenous leaders. In 2017, the average cost of supporting an indigenous church planter with Doulos Partners was $50 to $60 a month. While this amount may seem small to those of us in the West, this salary allows the indigenous church planter to live above the median income level in the country. This salary would allow the church planter to take care of the needs of their family, provide the necessary tools needed for ministry, and keep them from having to work multiple jobs to do so. With the amount of support being so affordable in terms of the resources found in the west, we are able to deploy more indigenous leaders to work the harvest field in their country. It allows us to be the best steward of the resources entrusted to us to reach the maximum number of people in the most cost-effective way.

A cautious word for those of us in America: we are the indigenous leaders here in our country. As we answer the call of Christ to reach the nations, we must also reach our own neighborhoods, cities, and states. We are constantly reminded by our brothers and sisters in other countries

44

that they are praying for us to be bold in our Jerusalem, Judea, and Samaria. Understanding that each of us is answering the call of Christ to take forth the gospel allows for a single-mindedness and unity that provides a synergy for the work.

This missions strategy creates a commonality between us that echoes that we are in this together for the sake of Christ.

> **God was leading us to empower indigenous believers to evangelize their own countrymen, disciple those new believers, and plant new churches.**

We want to affirm to the indigenous leader that we are not coming into their country to replace them in their mission to advance the Kingdom, but to empower them to do so. It shows that we are coming alongside them to enable them to even more powerfully answer the call of Christ to take the gospel forward. We have a common goal as we work together to see evangelism, discipleship, and church planting take place. We knew this would be the framework for our ministry. It was the most cost-efficient and the most effective way to reach the nations for Christ for which we were looking. God was leading us to empower indigenous believers to evangelize their own countrymen, disciple those new believers, and to plant new churches.

We do not deny the effective use of Western missionaries that are following God's call into service. You can walk in our homes and offices to find books on our shelves detailing the God ordained work of lives such as Jim and Elisabeth Elliot, Hudson Taylor, and Amy Carmichael. However, the Lord gave us a vision to invest in indigenous pastors to expand the Kingdom and to start building on the foundation of the last 200 years of the work that they, and so many others, have laid.

At Doulos, we have seen firsthand how the indigenous are one of the greatest assets that Jesus has given to make His name known. There are men and women all over the world right now, even as you read this very page, who are faithfully, tenaciously, courageously sharing the gospel of Jesus Christ. The invitation that Doulos Partners continues to extend is for you to actively be engaged in that work with them. We have surely seen over our ten years that the best people to reach the nations are the ones already living there!

SECTION 2

Making His Name Known:
The Partners

CHAPTER 4
World Link Ministries: Reaching Cuba

The Lord has used Wayne, Scott, and me to bring Doulos Partners the three different ministries that we work with in the field. He used Scott to bring us to our first partner. It was not necessarily the way we had it planned, but it was just the way that God worked it out. The first of these partners, as previously mentioned, was World Link Ministries from Dallas, Texas. To get a full picture of what took place, Scott will share his experience how God pointed him to this ministry and this country.

I wrestled with the best way to answer the call of God to take the gospel to the nations and how to start a ministry that would have an impact around the globe. The Lord brought Manny Fernandez to my mind. After setting up a phone conversation with Manny, I found out that he was the founder and CEO of World Link Ministries and he was very receptive to my call. He said that he would be coming to Birmingham the following week and would like to meet with Wayne and myself.

When we explained to Manny what we were envisioning, from a ministry perspective, he said: "We are already doing exactly what you're talking about." Immediately, Lev Bragg's advice came to mind: *Don't think you have to do something different than everyone else, just find someone who's already doing it well and join them.* It was starting to come together!

Manny was the first person I had ever seen or heard of that approached missions with a mindset of effectiveness being the singular driver behind every decision. We asked him how he dealt with church planters who were ineffective and he quickly replied, "I fire them!" That one sentence got my attention and convinced me that we needed to continue vetting them as a potential partner. We were "all in" to see this process through to completion!

Due to that meeting, we at MG&A were very excited about what we had seen and heard, and we decided to give a donation to World Link through our Doulos Foundation,

Cuba was a watershed moment in my life and I feel confident it was the same for everyone else on the trip.

which we sent to them in August of 2007. We now had an experienced ministry in the field in which we believed.

The planning started right away for us to visit Cuba, one of the countries in which World Link was working and where God was moving in an incredible way. This trip would be one of the last pieces of the puzzle we needed as we looked toward the possibility of a long-term relationship with World Link.

Our trip to Cuba included myself, Wayne, David, Mike Evans, Paul Head and Alan Dobbins. Other than David, the entire group was all executives from MG&A. Wayne and I were asking MG&A to make a three-year financial commitment to back Doulos and we felt like it was important that our key people be a part of that decision, so those guys going on the trip was a big deal. Cuba was a watershed moment in my life and I feel confident it was the same for everyone else on the trip.

What we experienced in Cuba was nothing like any of us had ever seen before. The Gospel was being preached and people were responding and being baptized. The churches shared what they had with each other, and the community and worship was authentic and spontaneous.

We were attending three services per day (during the week), and all were unique to their area and circumstances. It was an incredible time. When I called home, I told my wife that I had finally seen a true New Testament Church!

When we got back home, I was finally able to tell Davis that we were going on a mission trip. That summer, after the start of Doulos Partners and our decision to make World Link an official partner, I went back to Cuba with my family and it impacted their lives as much as it had mine and so many others. We were where God wanted us, doing what God wanted us to do. We would go back to Cuba two more times as a family, and Kelly would go back an additional time.

The last trip to Cuba we went on as a family was a very

special one. The Mountain People, as they are referred to in Cuba, were a unique group. Manny believed that the gospel had reached areas and pockets of this group of people, but he wasn't aware of any Americans that had gone into the mountains of Cuba for the purpose of preaching the gospel.

Our initial mountain trip consisted of Manny, myself, my sons Davis and Drew, their grandfather Doug Suggs, and Lev Bragg. We rode pack mules for four to five hours into the mountains, where we met up with our host family. Watching people live with no power, no running water, etc. was humbling to me. They had true joy in their lives and they were, and continue to be, an inspiration to me.

Our team brought them the international gift of baseball. Two gloves, a few brand new baseballs (a novelty in Cuba) and an aluminum bat—and within five minutes we had three 45- to 55-year-old men playing a game with smiles from ear to ear. They cooked and fed us meat they had harvested, and Manny explained the significance of that gesture. They were giving us their very best. Meat was a delicacy that they enjoyed sparingly, but you would have never known it by their attitudes and generosity.

That night we sat on the floor by candle light, in a three-room hut that housed two couples, and we shared stories of how Jesus had changed our lives. It was amazing to me that, even though I'd never met these people and didn't even understand their language, we all were really sharing the same stories about God's grace in our lives.

A few days later, we made a day trip into another mountain region, where my good friend Randy Overstreet joined us. We watched him perform baptisms in one of the most beautiful waterfalls I've ever seen. There have been some amazing times in Cuba and, in ten lifetimes, I wouldn't be able to thank Manny Fernandez enough for his personal influence in my life and for his willingness to be available during the most critical times of Doulos Partners' beginnings. I certainly didn't realize at the time the impact our first meeting would have on my life, my family's lives, and my friend's lives, but I see it clearly now and I will be forever grateful.

Since our initial trip in 2008, through God's grace and His allowing us to be a part of supporting those on the ground in Cuba, as well as the church planters in the other 35 countries that we serve in we have seen over five million people make a profession of faith in Christ while seeing over 19,000 churches planted. To God be the glory for the great things He has done!

CHAPTER 5
Cuba: The Stories of the Faithful

Cuba is a unique place. Sometimes called the "Pearl of the Caribbean," it is an island of great beauty—and great hardship.

The people are warm and generous, but they live in extreme poverty. They are incarcerated in their own county, but our believing brothers and sisters exhibit such joy and freedom. As it has always been with the movement of the gospel, the church flourishes most under struggle and persecution.

Let these stories give you hope and encouragement, as they do me.

Eduardo's Story

• • •

"Eduardo," as we will call him, was a successful, highly decorated tank commander in the army. The government asked him to attend a church as an undercover agent to ensure that the church was not speaking out against them and calling for a revolt.

In duty to his country, Eduardo got up one Sunday morning and went to the church. The pastor was preaching a powerful message on sin and the need for a savior in order to be reconciled to God. He very clearly shared the gospel from the birth of Christ to His death and resurrection.

It was there, as an undercover plant, that Eduardo heard the message of the gospel for the very first time. He thought he was there to keep everything in check and to make sure that the church was operating within the limits that the government had provided, but God had a different plan that morning. Instead, Eduardo came face to face with the understanding that he was a sinner and could not save himself. When the pastor extended the invitation, this agent for the government stood up and walked forward to publicly profess his faith in Jesus.

The pastor began to disciple Eduardo and encourage him on his walk with Christ. Not too long after that, Eduardo resigned his commission in the army and walked away from his government position to continue deeper training and discipleship with the pastor who had shared eternal life with him. It was during this time that the Lord called Eduardo to become a pastor and church planter.

During my first trip to Cuba, I had the opportunity to visit with Eduardo and attend the church that met in his home. I listened as the people in his church told story after story of how the Lord had used Eduardo to change the lives of his family and his neighbors, and to help plant twelve new churches.

Two years later, I was back in Eduardo's home to preach and teach. I was encouraged to see that the twelve churches that God had started through him were still multiplying and replicating, and had grown to 26 church plants.

Several years later, I was back once again—this time, at a training for our church planters. I looked up to see Eduardo. We embraced as brothers as if seeing each other at a homecoming after spending years apart. I asked him then how many churches the Lord had birthed out of the one that was started in his living room years before. With a joy in his eyes, he said that they had started a total of 77 churches, and he was excited to report that they were all thriving. Wow, what a picture of transformation and multiplication.

Antonio's Story

•   •   •

On my first trip to the island of Cuba, I met a pastor in his early 70s who we will call Antonio. On the outside, Antonio looked like a cantankerous old man. In reality, he was full of energy, life, and love for everyone around him. His compassion for the people and excitement for the gospel gave him a desire to be useful, constantly setting up for services, coordinating details and even cheering on the kids playing baseball in the field across the street.

One night, we were preparing for an outdoor baptism service for about 30 people. It was like nothing I had ever experienced before. I walked out and saw a rough, hand-dug hole in the ground lined with concrete blocks. It had been filled with water. It was Antonio who had taken care of all of these details. I was curious to learn more about him, and so I asked a lot of questions about his life and journey.

Antonio grew up as a tough street kid. At twelve years old, he was regularly carrying a handgun. It was about this time in his life that one of his friends invited him to go to church, and after some convincing, Antonio decided he would attend. He heard about Jesus for the very first time and accepted Him as his savior.

He was hungry not only for his spiritual growth, but to find ways that he could be helpful in the life of the church. He soon learned that, like himself, many of his fellow believers did not have Bibles or any way to purchase them. So, he devised a plan. He used his gun and robbed a bakery in town. With the money he stole, he bought Bibles for the church. Problem solved!

The pastor applauded him for his enthusiasm but corrected his method. The more mature believers took the time to help Antonio make amends with the bakery owner and then continued to mentor him. He soon developed an understanding of being a new creation and allowing the old ways of his life to pass away.

Antonio continued to grow in his walk with Jesus and finished his training. Then, he became a pastor of a church in Cuba. The commander (much like our mayor) of his city would often call him in to question him about the ministries of the church or give him orders on what he could and could not do as a pastor. As you can imagine, this never sat well with a former tough street kid. After weeks filled with intense conversations with the commander, another summons was issued. He prepared himself for what could come that day. Antonio knew this meeting would not be easy.

As he neared the office, he saw a big rock in a flowerbed. Antonio looked down and picked it up to carry it in with him. When he walked in the door, the commander was shocked by the sight of the rock, and questioned Antonio's intentions, implying that the plan might be to hurt him.

While assuring the commander he meant no harm, Antonio very calmly, but with fierce determination, dropped it on the desk and said, "It does not matter what you do to me. Even the rocks will cry out to the love and forgiveness of Jesus Christ." In the face of adversity and persecution, Antonio stood on the promises of the one, true, living God that had called him from death to life and into the pastoral ministry.

Isn't it interesting to see how Antonio grew from milk to meat? May that be our testimonies as well.

Bernardo's Story

• • •

On a trip to Cuba in late 2008, I met a young man who we will call Yates and his mother, Rosa. Yate's dad, Bernardo, who had died several years earlier, had a strong belief in Jesus. He was involved in the church alongside his wife but he felt that he had not been very productive in advancing the kingdom. When Bernardo was 77 years old, he came to Manny Fernandez and asked to be trained by the World Link team, both theologically and practically so that he could become a preacher, evangelist, and church planter.

Manny was stunned by this request. The typical church planter that they hired and trained was much younger with the ability to do many years of work and ministry. As a matter of fact, Manny told him that World Link was not in the "geriatric" ministry and did not believe that this was a good investment of the ministry's time or resources.

Bernardo continued to state his case. He explained that he was a decorated war hero, fought in the Bay of Pigs and had a chest full of medals. However, he said that none of his efforts or accolades had put any money in his pocket or a single loaf of bread on his table. Bernardo went on to compare this with his walk with the Lord. He said that even though he had done some things for the Kingdom, fought some battles and accomplished some victories, it was not enough, not nearly enough. His desire was to enter heaven knowing he had given everything left in his life toward making Jesus's name known in his part of

Cuba. He really did not have much fruit, if any, and that he did not want to stand before Jesus when he got to heaven empty-handed.

Manny and the other leaders were moved by this man's heart. They decided to invest in him and train him. At 77 years old, this man began to use the years he had left to advance the Kingdom.

Bernardo went to be with the Lord at the age of 81. In those four years, he had the opportunity to lead between 200 and 300 people to faith in Christ while starting five new churches. This was a man who was at a time in his life where many, if not most, are retired.

He could have said as most do, "I have done my time, let someone else do this job." Instead, he wanted to use every day he had left to build the Kingdom so that one day he could hear those words from Jesus: "Well done, my good and faithful servant."

Nowhere in the Bible does it say that we should retire from serving the Lord after a certain age, and Bernardo showed that example. His faithfulness of serving until the end has led to work that is continuing to flourish until this day. Well done, Bernardo. Thank you for finishing strong!

Jose's Story

• • •

In 2013, a team of six of us flew into Havana late on a Saturday night. The next morning, we ate some breakfast and left the hotel heading west to join a group of 29 new church congregations for worship and Bible Study. One of our team members asked about the leadership on the island and Manny replied by telling us the story of Jose, which, as you probably expect, is not his real name.

Jose was a church planter with World Link. He was committed to doing everything he could to reach his countrymen with the gospel, and he had a heart for seeing this island come to know Jesus.

Anytime he learned of a person who felt called to the ministry, Jose would disciple them. His team grew rapidly, and together, they had planted about 200 churches.

As he observed continued growth among the new believers, Jose felt like there needed to be a training center. In his mind, it would be a place where church plants could bring groups of new believers for discipleship as well as a place for church planters to continue their theological studies for Kingdom work.

With limited resources available, Jose, his wife, and his four children moved out of their home and into one room in the home of his in-laws. Think about this for a second: this man took his family out of their home, and the six of them lived in a small bedroom where they all slept on the floor. They did this so that their house could be used as a place for a church plant to meet, a training center for new believers, and a central location for continuing education for church planters. How many people do you know that would make that kind of sacrifice to advance the gospel?

As Manny finished telling us this story, we arrived at our destination and looked up to see a man in the middle of the road waving his arms. It was Jose. He was showing us the place to stop and park so that we could join the worship service.

As the service was coming to a close, an invitation was given and a number of people came forward.
Suddenly, there was a commotion that caught my attention. I looked across the crowd and saw an old woman shouting and walking toward the front with tears streaming down her face and, at the same time, I saw Jose with tears running down his face and literally sprinting toward her. As he reached her he shouted, "*Mi mamá, mi mamá.*"

For 17 years, Jose had been praying for his mother to come to faith in Jesus. That day, we were able to see the answer to the faithful prayers of a son on behalf of his mom. Those are the unexpected things that we get to witness in the field when we are faithful to go.

Pablo's Story

• • •

I had the chance to interview some of the new church planters in Cuba who had been trained and were ready to be deployed for full-time work. This is how I met Pablo.

Pablo was a professional grass cutter in Cuba by day, and was a financially un-supported church planter by night and on the weekends. He described his schedule for me: He would rise early, get dressed, grab his machete, and go out to hand cut grass on the side of the road. He did this until midafternoon, when he had met his government quota for the day. He took his portion for his farm animals and stacked the rest of the grass for a government worker to come by and pick it up later in the day.

He would then go home, get cleaned up and eat a meal. Then, his day as a church planter would begin. He would go back out into the community to preach the gospel and disciple new believers.

I asked him questions about his faith and he shared that he had only been a Christian for eight months. I stood in amazement as he shared with me that in that very short amount of time, the Lord had given him the opportunity to lead 400 people to Christ and plant eight new churches.

This young man had a deep desire to see the gospel go forward and told me that he was asking the Lord to provide a salary for him so that he could stop cutting grass in order to be a full-time church planter. He felt that the call on his life was not to be a harvester of grass for the

Cuban government, but a harvester of souls for the Kingdom of God.

Pablo was hired that day. He was then able to leave his grass-cutting job and begin planting churches full time. He continues to faithfully preach, teach, and train new leaders to take the gospel across the island.

I was thrilled that we were able to help this young man realize his calling, but my heart is heavy knowing there are thousands more who are trained, willing, and able, for which we still have no funding. It is very comforting to know that the Lord knows all of our needs and will supply them in His timing.

However, I am glad that we got to see this first hand in Pablo's life! Praise God!

66

Thomas Minor, Chairman of the Board, baptizes new believers in Cuba.

As Scott mentioned, a baseball game broke out in the mountains of Cuba as we started to get to know them.

The very first trip to Cuba in February 2008, with Mike Evans, David Johnson, Wayne Myrick, Manny Fernandez, Paul Head, John Bell, Scott Gurosky, and Alan Dobbins.

Kelly Gurosky working with one of the local church plants hosting a Vacation Bible School.

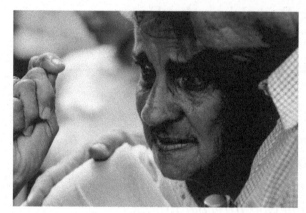

A picture of Jose embracing his mother immediately after her profession of faith as mentioned on page 62.

Junior Board Member, Patrick Dreher, baptizing a believer in Cuba after finishing a year-long discipleship program.

CHAPTER 6
Biglife: Reaching the East

As I noted at the beginning of Chapter 4, the Lord used all three of us in different ways and at different times to lead us to our three partners. God clearly used Wayne to show us His will about our second partnership, Biglife. Here is Wayne's account of how God directed him.

Our company, MG&A, designed and constructed phase II of First Baptist Church Naples, Florida, and that is where I met Jim Evans. Jim was a temporary church administrator filling in during a time of transition for the church. Jim and I grew to be good friends and I had a lot of respect for him after working with him for nearly three years. It's unusual to find someone of Jim's business experience and spiritual maturity in that role. I was very fortunate to have met Jim Evans and to have seen the relationship and walk that he had with God.

Shortly after Doulos Partners' beginning, towards the

end of 2008, we started discussing the possibility of a second partner. Alan Dobbins and I had previously attended a fundraising event in Naples, Florida, for Biglife, a ministry that was working with indigenous church planters in the eastern part of the world. It was there that we met John Heerema, the Executive Director, Jim Evan's son Jim, Jr., who was then a volunteer and is now the CFO and Jeff Gibson, who was their VP of Development at the time and is now their president.

After meeting Jim Jr., it was clear that the apple certainly didn't fall far from the tree. I was very impressed with what I had heard and seen, it was a serious ministry effort. So, when David, Scott & I started talking about another partner, Biglife was the first thing on my mind.

David and I decided to go to Naples, Florida and have lunch with John, Jim Jr., and Jeff to discuss the ministry. It seems sometimes that God is perfectly navigating our life experiences, and this was one of those times. It was clear that our strategy of using indigenous leaders was already being implemented through this ministry.

Everything we talked about that day lined up with our mission, and so we agreed that it would be worthwhile to continue our vetting of the ministry by going to the field to see the work for ourselves. So in the spring of 2009, I traveled to the state of West Bengal with Jim Jr. and Jeff for a ten-day trip to see first-hand what Biglife was doing in India and how their plan was executed.

The city of Kolkata was central for the effort of Biglife. They had built an impressive network of ministry

> It was clear that our strategy of using indigenous leaders was already being implemented through this ministry.

leaders and church planters over the five years of their work.

When we landed at the airport there, we were picked up and driven to the William Carey house, where we stayed in a dormitory for visiting mission teams. You could walk out of the fenced property and buy chai tea on every street corner. I didn't particularly care for it, but it seemed to be very popular.

Benjamin Francis was the Biglife in-country Director. His previous vocation was in banking. It didn't take long to see the tremendous work ethic and organizational skills that he displayed. Sometimes mission trips can turn into vacation/sightseeing trips, but this was certainly not the case here. While we were in Kolkata, we were a part of organized large group events and sports or game activities that would culminate in gospel presentations. There were church planters present, and they would take all those who had become believers and start gathering as churches immediately. There were always enough people to make a good start at meeting and studying the Bible.

We would do a couple of these events during the day and also go to several small group meetings in homes along the way. In most of these gatherings, we would baptize new believers. Each person baptized would get a certificate and also sign a statement certifying their intentions.

These certificates were given to the church planters so that they could keep records of all who were baptized. They could then start the disciple-making process in a local church plant. There was no dead time during the day or evening. The days were long and the nights were short. We would rise early, always to the unnerving sound of the Muslim call to prayer, which blared on the loud speakers throughout the city five times a day. We fell into our beds late at night, exhausted.

After several days of work in Kolkata, we left for the northern border of India along the Padma River that separates India from Bangladesh. We then traveled north to the city of Siliguri. I will never forget 18 hours on a pre-World War II train. I am not sure if there was heating or cooling on the train but I do remember it was a miserable way to travel. Each car had a hole in the floor for obvious reasons. The trains were always packed with people. I soon learned why Jim Jr. and Jeff only brought a backpack. I am lucky that I had only one suitcase, but it wasn't as easy as the backpack.

We spent several days going from village to village with the same format as in Kolkata and with similar success.

We did have some interesting encounters with Imams, which are the leaders of the Mosques. They were always close by and watching us with intensity. Because of the discernment of the church planters, who knew who to approach and what to say, we were able to navigate the atmosphere of confrontation safely.

Typically, the team would pull up to a large public area

or village, and within a short while, there would be a crowd. They would have some fun activities for the children and the parents who were soon gathered in to watch. Then the church planters would share their witness for Christ, often using the Quran to give credibility. What most people do not know is that Jesus is mentioned in that book as "the only one who knows the way to heaven." Almost without fail, many would accept Christ and a new church body was formed. They would do this two or three times a day. I was amazed at how effortless it seemed to be. The days were long and tiring, but it never seemed like it was work to them. This is nothing like the United States.

An interesting event occurred in one of the villages. A woman, who had accepted Christ, wanted us to help her rid her house of all the idols of her Hindu past, of which there were so many! We actually threw them all in a river. This made some of the people in her village extremely upset.

I wish it were that easy to dispose of our idols in America.

After three days, we went back to Kolkata to cover the outer areas of the city, working closely with Benjamin. We traveled through the mountains from village to village, meeting people in the churches they had planted. One day, we took a 100-mile trip in our Tata SUV, (Tata is the largest vehicle manufacturer in India). We started in the morning and met the local leader in a village about 20 miles outside of Kolkata. We met six teenagers in our first gathering. As we traveled on, from time to time, they would show up at other villages and meetings that were planned for the day. We saw them at our final meeting and discovered that they had traveled by foot or by getting rides along the way.

They had followed us all day to hear scriptures read and taught. Can you imagine anyone in America doing that? It left a lasting impression on me.

Our last day in India was spent with Benjamin in several of their larger congregations, and then we had time to review our travels and experiences. It was obvious to us that the key to reaching the world with the gospel was just what we had seen in those previous days, and it would be done with people just like the ones we had met and spent time with. I believed we had found our next partner because of the way they approached God's call to make disciples.

Biglife had the leadership, the network established, accountability processes and excellent record-keeping. They weren't afraid to terminate people if need be. This was a serious ministry effort with serious people. We saw the Gospel call being given and answered hourly over the eight days we were in country.

Since that beginning they have started new work in countries like Nepal, Pakistan, Afghanistan, Bangladesh, Cambodia, Vietnam, and many others. Recently Doulos has partnered with Biglife to start the same process in various refugee camps that have sprung up due to the growth of ISIS in the Middle East. This ministry is a joy to work with and we are thankful for the tenacity in which they serve the Lord and carry out their mission.

CHAPTER 7
Central and Southeast Asia:
The Stories of the Faithful

In this area of the world, it is very dangerous to be a Christ-follower. The church planters that we support in these countries are putting their lives on the line every day for the advancement of the Kingdom. In fact, 51 of them have been killed in the last five years.

The stories you are about to read all have some level of persecution, martyrdom, or difficulty. As you enter in to these people's lives, my prayer is that you will have a sense of awe at the way that the Lord has worked, and that you would have a renewed commitment to put your "everything" on the line! Please join with me in praying for these incredible men and women.

Faizal's Story

• • •

In one of my earliest meetings with John Heerema in 2009, he told me the story of their first leader in Pakistan named Faizal.

Faizal grew up in a radical extremist Muslim family. They were devoted to following the Islamic tradition. They were well respected and involved in every area of the mosque and Muslim religion.

Faizal was recruited by Al Qaeda to be enlisted and trained as a fighter in the jihadist movement. In this country and culture, it was an honor for the mosque, the family, and the community to have one of your own chosen to be a fighter for Al Qaeda.

Faizal left his home and went to the tribal area where the training would take place. There, he was taught everything he needed to know to be an Al Qaeda member.

According to protocol, at the end of the training, before your first assignment, you are sent home. At this time, you would see your family and attend your mosque to be honored and celebrated before going on the first assignment.

After his time at home, Faizal began his journey back to the camp and stopped for tea. As he sat down on a bench, the wind started to pick up.

Paper and trash were blowing all around him with the exception of one piece of paper. It was lying perfectly still on the ground and not being affected by the strong wind. It appeared to have a bright light shining on it. He reached out and grabbed the piece of paper and began to read. On it was written Matthew 5:9, *"Blessed are the peacemakers, for they shall be called the sons of God."*

Even throughout his training in the Al Qaeda camp, he had begun to question the idea of Islam, and something just didn't seem right. After being trained to be a killer, seeing on this slip of paper about being a peacemaker made Faizal want to know more.

It was then that he remembered a man who had once talked to him about Jesus. He took the piece of paper back to this man and asked him what it meant.

The man opened the Bible to Matthew to walk him through the life of Jesus and a presentation of the gospel. Faizal gave his life to the Lord. Immediately, this man connected Faizal with a church planter with Biglife for extended discipleship.

It was through this relationship that Faizal became the leader of the Kingdom work that was taking place across the country of Pakistan.

During one of the early meetings between Faizal and the Biglife leadership, he made a firm commitment to go throughout Pakistan and even to the Al Qaeda camps to reach the lost for Jesus.

His request was that when (not if, but when) he was killed, that they would help take care of his wife and children.

This one statement showed that Faizal had counted the cost and was ready to move forward for the sake of the gospel.

Since that moment on his journey back to the Al Qaeda camp when the Holy Spirit used that piece of paper, Faizal has been a part of seeing over 6,000 professions of faith and helped plant 1,125 churches.

Tapashi's Story

• • •

In 2010, I took my first trip to India. On our first day, we went out to a village outside the city of Kolkata and, as we entered, we started playing games with the children. As the children came, their moms were not far behind. The fathers would slowly move in to the outside edge of the circle to watch.

The games taught Bible stories of Abraham and Noah and the Ark, and soon the moms were participating. When the men saw that there was no harm being done, they would eventually come closer.

As I often do when I am in the field, I watched the leaders participating in the outreach efforts. One young woman, probably in her late twenties, dressed in the traditional Indian style, drew my attention. Just by looking into her eyes, you could sense her sweet, genuine spirit.

A few days later, we were in Kolkata participating in some training of our church planters and I saw her again. On our last day, I was in the home of one of our regional leaders in India to preach at the house church that met there. For the third time during our trip, I saw the young woman again. After finishing up the service, I knew that I had to get a picture with her. Rarely when you are traveling in country do you see the same person that many times, and it made me curious. After getting our picture made and saying our good byes, one of the other church leaders came up and asked if I knew her story. Of course,

I knew nothing more than the short introductions that we exchanged.

He said her name was Tapashi (ta-PAH-she) and she was once a village prostitute. Her husband was the one who was selling her into prostitution. One day, one of our church planters came to her village where they met her for the first time. Tapashi spent some time listening to them that morning and watching the games with the children. She decided to come back that evening to see *The Jesus Film*. Tapashi heard the Gospel presented and knew right away that she was a sinner in need of a savior. That night, Tapashi came to know the Lord.

Immediately, she went to her husband to share with him that she could no longer be a prostitute.

Here is a woman who had just heard the Gospel clearly presented for the first time and does not own a Bible, but she knows that after coming to faith in Christ that she can no longer go back to her old life. While she didn't know the verse that proclaims, *"If anyone is in Christ, he is a new creation. The old has passed away; behold, the new has come,"* in her heart, she knew that truth. She knew something was different.

Upon hearing her confession of faith and rejection of the lifestyle that they were living, he beat her and took her before the tribal council. The council's judgment was to affirm the decision of her husband and require her to obey him. If she chose not to do so, they would shave her head and she would become a village outcast. She immediately found other believers in her village and she asked the church planter to come and pray with her for her husband. After spending this time in prayer and seeking wisdom from other believers, Tapashi went back to her husband a second time.

With her cuts and bruises still visible from the last beating, Tapashi faced him. She told him that she could no longer be a prostitute. She again confessed that she had fully given her life to Jesus Christ who had lived and died for the sins of the world and was ready to take whatever worldly consequences he had for her including becoming a village outcast. She also shared with him that the same Jesus that had saved her was willing to do the same for him.

This conversation was very different. You see, the Holy Spirit had gone before her and prepared the soil of her husband's heart. That day, her husband accepted Jesus Christ as his Lord and Savior.

Together, they have worked with the Biglife team and have been a part of starting churches in some 15 different villages.

Tapan's Story

• • •

In September of 2011, I made my second trip to India with Doulos Partners. When I arrived, I was asked by the Biglife regional leader, Benjamin Francis, to teach Revelation 1, 2, and 3 to a group of church planters in the area. He wanted for his group to focus not on the quantity of churches, but the quality of churches that were being planted. After spending eight hours teaching, one of those in attendance named Tapan approached me to show his appreciation. As I often do when in these situations, I asked Tapan to tell me his story.

Tapan and his wife came from a traditional Hindu background. Their marriage was an arranged one, as many of them are in their culture. In 2006, he became very sick. His family tried everything they knew to help him. The doctors came, but no medicine could heal him. The Hindu priests came and performed sacrifices by his bedside, but he continued to get worse. His family brought in the village witch doctors and they danced around him even as his health deteriorated.

Finally, the doctor looked at Tapan's father and told him to prepare for Tapan's death. When one of the family members heard this, they went to his father and told him about a man who lived in the area who had prayed over people and seen them healed. Fearing his son's impending death, his father asked no questions and sent them to find him.

This man prayed over Tapan, asking Jesus to come and

to heal his body. Tapan went to bed and when he woke up the next morning, he was completely healed. After this experience, he asked to see the man again. You see, it was one of our church planters with Biglife that was summoned to Tapan's bedside. The church planter came back to Tapan's home and there he shared that it was not him, but Jesus who brought healing. Through their conversations, Tapan and his wife came to know the Lord Jesus as their Savior. They immediately began to tell everyone they could about the one who saved them, Jesus. He had no training, no Bible, and no church background, but Tapan knew that he had to tell of what Jesus had done in his life.

Regardless of the obvious healing, Tapan's family began to persecute him and his wife, telling them that they must recant their profession of faith in Christ and return to Hinduism. Even as they continued to apply pressure and reject them, Tapan and his wife said that they would never deny their faith.

Tapan became a church planter with Biglife. In 2008, he was out in another village preaching and received a call on his cell phone. (Yes- even some of the most remote and impoverished areas in the world have access to cellular technology.) The person on the other end of the phone said Tapan's wife was very sick and he needed to come home. Tapan got on his bike and rode as quickly as possible.

He said, "Pastor David, I rode up my street and there was a huge crowd of people in front of my house. As I turned in, people started to split, like the Red Sea parted for Moses and the people of Israel. There I saw my wife, dead and hanging from a tree in my front yard."

I will never forget his next words to me. Tapan said, "It was that moment where God said to me that I was not to have a spirit of anger, resentment or retaliation. You are to extend mercy, grace and forgiveness to your wife's killers."

He would come to find out later that it was his parents and his in-laws who were the ones responsible.

God continued to remind Tapan that while the culture says to retaliate, he should forgive just as he had been forgiven. And with God's help, Tapan did just that. In the three years since his wife's murder, Tapan had the opportunity to see 23 family members come to Christ including his parents and in-laws who had put his wife to death. John Heerema had the privilege to be at the baptism service where Tapan baptized his mother-in-law and father-in-law. They came out of the baptismal waters weeping over their sin and the power of forgiveness.

From 2008 to that point in 2011, the Lord had used Tapan and his team to plant 137 churches. This is probably one of the greatest stories on forgiveness that I have ever heard. It is amazing to know that the Lord forgives us and when we obediently forgive, it changes the lives of others.

Village Number 273

• • •

On one of our trips to India, we traveled to the area of the South 24 Parganas (PAR-gah-nas). This area contains many islands that cannot be reached any other way than by water. Several years ago, our partner Biglife, purchased a boat for the purpose of getting access to these people groups with the gospel.

On this trip, two of the indigenous leaders helped us board the boat and begin our journey to one of the islands. As we made our way through the water, they described for us the ministry in this area.

There were about 900 villages on 57 islands, and today we would be visiting number 273 on the list they had compiled. They were meticulous with their planning to ensure that they were able to reach each and every island and village. As we landed, I, along with two of our board members, Lev Bragg and Gregg Morrison, got out of the boat and followed one of the church planters into the village to meet the Chief. He and his family welcomed us into their hut and began to serve us some tea. It was then that I noticed that the Chief's son was wearing a shiny cross necklace. Through an interpreter, I asked him about it.

He had purchased it while he was visiting a neighboring village just because it was interesting and pretty, but he had no idea of the meaning. Our indigenous brothers are always alert to even the slightest opportunity to bring the gospel into every circumstance, and this was no exception. Benjamin Francis immediately turned to me and asked me to share the gospel with those in the hut. It was the first time in my life to share the gospel with a group of people who had no context or frame of reference for the gospel. The people around me had never before heard the name of Jesus.

In that moment a fear came over me. While I had shared the gospel many times in many different venues, I had no idea where to begin. In the midst of my panic, the Lord calmly and quietly said "Creation, The Fall, and Redemption." I started with the beginning and walked through creation, how He not only created us but sustains us. I moved to the fall of man that brought sin to the earth and, in turn, separated man from God. Even on man's best day, he is unworthy of being brought before a Holy God. Man needed a Savior and God sent His son, Jesus. Redemption is only possible through Him.

It was so exciting to see the Chief, who was in his early 80s, come to faith in Christ. He told us that he had been waiting his entire life to have someone tell him this story.

This experience continues to remind me that our call to take the gospel into the world is as important today as it has ever been. There are still people who have never heard the good news of Jesus and have been waiting for someone to come and share it. If we don't go, who will?

Deiu Sanh's Story

• • •

I have had the privilege of making two trips to the country of Cambodia. On my first trip there, I had the opportunity to travel to a small town on the Cambodia/Vietnam border. We had tried to get visas into Vietnam, but we were denied. We were so disappointed, thinking we may not get a chance to meet the Vietnamese church planters. Ever resourceful and tenacious, ten of these men traveled nine hours on mopeds into Cambodia.

We gathered together in a small room in our hotel. Communicating with an incredible language barrier proved difficult, as our conversations had to be translated from English to Khmer (KA-meer) to Vietnamese and back again the same way.

We laughed as we talked about our longing for the day in heaven when we would all be able to communicate together without this struggle.

One of the church planters we will call Deiu Sanh (DAY-san) had come to know Christ and had begun to faithfully preach the gospel in some of the more remote villages in Vietnam. Because of his preaching, Deiu Sanh had been arrested three times and spent a total of 13 years in prison. As he said this, everyone around the room began to nod their heads in affirmation as they had all been in prison at least once for the preaching of the gospel.

During the last of his imprisonments, Deiu Sanh was called into the warden's office. The warden wanted to know if he would stop preaching once he was released from prison. You see, during all three imprisonments, Deiu Sanh had continued to cause trouble, preaching to any other prisoner with whom he came in contact.

Deiu Sanh looked at the warden and told him with conviction that, even if he was released, he would continue to preach. The warden was unhappy, but not particularly surprised by this answer. He wanted Deiu Sanh's relentless preaching out of his facility, but he knew it wouldn't be long before he was brought right back again.

The solution to his dilemma was unorthodox, but effective. He had arranged for Deiu Sanh to be given a special certificate. This document would allow for him to travel anywhere in the country of Vietnam and preach the good news of Jesus Christ. The warden went on to tell Deiu Sanh that as long as he had the certificate with him, he could present it to anyone who questioned him to show he had authority from the Vietnamese government to preach the gospel.

After spending 13 years in prison, they were now giving him permission to do the very thing for which he had been arrested so many times. We stood amazed. This could only have been done by God! We enjoyed our time with the church planters and could see the joy of the Lord on each of their faces. This was especially true as I looked at Deiu Sanh. Here was a man who was a modern-day Paul; preaching the gospel even while he was in prison. A few years later, we were able to receive visas into Vietnam. Meeting with some of the church planters in the country, we could tell that something was wrong.

Deiu Sanh's daughter, Seyon (SAY-yon), had been abducted.

Deiu Sanh, along with some of the brothers and sisters in the city, were frantically searching for her. They knew that those who were trafficking young women would try to get her out of the country as quickly as possible and time was of the essence.

Finding Deiu Sanh's daughter certainly took precedent over everything else so we changed our plan and left Vietnam. We went to Cambodia to visit with the church planters there and see more of the work in that country. Even so, our hearts were heavy with the thought of Deiu Sanh and his daughter. We returned home without any news of her being found, but continued to pray for the Lord to work in ways only He can for her good and safety.

For six months, we prayed and waited for news. Then one day, we received a call that Seyon had been miraculously rescued. We learned that Thi Nhem (Thī Nim), Deiu Sanh's wife, went to bed praying as she always did, for the protection and rescue of her daughter. Her fervent hope was that she would see her daughter again. That night, she had a dream. She saw the front of an unfamiliar building and she heard the voice of the Lord telling her that Seyon was in that very place. She immediately woke up, called for Deiu Sanh and began to describe the building she had seen in her dream.

Deiu Sanh said he knew the building she spoke of. He gathered some of the brothers to go there. The building appeared vacant. However, when they entered through the back, they found Seyon tucked away in a closet.

While she had been through more than any of us can imagine, the Lord had saved her life and brought rescue through a vision to her mother. Seyon now goes village to village alongside her father, sharing of how the Lord sustained her and saved her. Seyon has used this horrific experience to share about the love of Christ and how only He can bring true rescue.

Bittu's Story

• • •

My first three trips to India were all on the eastern side of the country, with Kolkata as the base of our work. For many years, this was the extent of my knowledge about this vast area. However, on my fourth trip, I had the opportunity to visit the state of Punjab, which is in the northwest part of the country close to the Pakistani border.

I was impressed with the attention to detail and the passion the leaders had for the Kingdom work that was taking place there. Just by speaking to them, you could hear their desire.

They understood the importance of training church planters well and sending them out for the work. It was there, while doing theological training, that I had the opportunity to meet a man by the name of Bittu (Bi-TOO). I noticed him right away because he walked in the room wearing dark glasses and holding the arm of an older man. I realized that Bittu was blind. At one of the breaks, I asked him to tell me his story.

Growing up, Bittu had no desire to become a Christian even though some of his family members had come to follow Jesus. He wanted nothing to do with religion or the things of God. He was a tough man, and he spent time as a member of a gang in the area.

A landowner hired Bittu and his gang to throw some squatters off his land. A terrible fight broke out. Bittu picked up a rock and struck a woman with it. She fell to the ground bleeding and her husband pulled out a gun and fired it at Bittu. He said he felt like his entire face was on fire. His fellow gang members grabbed him and took him to the hospital, where he spent three days with the doctors and nurses unsuccessfully trying to stop the bleeding.

A Biglife pastor had been trying to reach out to Bittu for the last several months. When he heard what had happened, he came to see him in the hospital. He laid hands on Bittu and prayed in the name of Jesus, and immediately the bleeding stopped. Bittu laid in the hospital that night, pondering all that happened and what he had experienced at the hand of this pastor. He finally fell asleep, and Jesus appeared to him in a dream.

Bittu explained to me that even though he was blind, he saw Jesus standing in his room with a bright light surrounding him. Jesus said to him, "Bittu, I am who others have said that I am and I have come with a great work for you to do."

He gave his life to Jesus and had a great sense of urgency about the task that was set before him. He started his mission by sharing his story and the saving power of Jesus with his family. One of the first people to hear his testimony and come to faith was his father, the same man I saw leading Bittu into the room that day. Since becoming Christians, Bittu and his father have been ministry partners, traveling from village to village proclaiming the name of Jesus. It was such a cool picture to see Bittu on the back of a bicycle with his dad peddling away.

Several years later, I had the opportunity to travel back to Punjab and see Bittu again. Just as it was the first time, he came into the room being led by his father. As they walked in, there was a warmth that came with them. It was as if the entire room could feel the presence of the Holy Spirit.

As they sat down, Bittu was called on to open our time together in prayer. While I don't have any idea of what he said in his native tongue, I had a oneness of heart with him because of the connection we have in Christ. There was such power in his prayer. It was as if all of heaven came down and was with us. It was such a God moment.

Times like these are etched in my mind as I think about this man, who cannot see physically but has 20/20 vision spiritually. His full surrender to serve Jesus has continued to inspire me, even now, as we hear reports of the fruitfulness of his ongoing ministry.

Klem's Story

• • •

Flying into Cambodia on our first trip there, I was greeted at the airport by two men that we will call Vannak (Va Nock) and Klem.

Upon meeting Klem, you could sense that there was something special about him. He had the gift of service and daily tried to find ways to help make our time in the country easy and enjoyable. A few days into the trip, I had the opportunity to meet his family and found out that Klem was HIV positive.

Many years earlier, as he became sick, Klem was estranged from his family. When he was in the hospital, Vannak came to see him and shared the gospel with him. There in his hospital room he prayed to receive Christ. Shortly after, his body went into remission and he became healthier. He left the hospital and was reunited with his wife and children. From that point forward, Klem and his family committed themselves to the work of the Kingdom. At the time I was visiting with him, he had been a part of the team that planted 135 churches in the area.

On my second trip, I was able to see Klem again. I was told that the rest of his family had contracted the disease. I also found out that Klem liked to carve wood: beautiful pieces of crosses and of blocks carved into the name of Jesus. As he was telling me about his art, he beamed with joy at the gift that God had given him. After the service, Klem brought out some of his completed pieces for us to see. Tofey Leon, a board member and dear friend, was with us on the trip. He and I decided to purchase all of the carvings that he had made. His face lit up as he saw our excitement on being able to take his work home to share with our family and friends.

We returned home and not long after, I received a prayer gram from Biglife that alerted us that the HIV was causing major issues for Klem. Soon, an e-mail arrived that Klem had passed away. I mourned the loss of our brother, while at the same time rejoicing that he was face to face with Jesus.

Klem's wife and children are still doing well and continue to be a part of the Kingdom work in Cambodia. She has been able to start a food cart to support the ongoing needs of her family. While they miss Klem, they know that he is without pain and is rejoicing with his Savior in heaven. It always amazes me how the Lord uses people from the most unlikely places to touch our lives.

I really look forward to seeing my friend and brother in heaven. His smile was contagious and his heart pure. That work continues on today and over 360 churches have been planted there at the time of this book's publishing.

Signs and Wonders

• • •

In April of 2014, I had the opportunity to go to Nepal with Benjamin Francis and some of the Biglife team. We met with 50 church planters that traveled from their villages in some of the most remote parts of the Himalayan mountains across extremely difficult terrain. During breaks in our teaching time, I had the chance to step outside and hear their testimonies as they shared them with our team.

As I listened, spellbound, to these men and women, I realized, more than ever, that Jesus doesn't *need* me. He *allows* me the privilege to participate in the work that He is doing.

With every testimony, I was reminded that signs and wonders are still taking place around the world. God is still raising people from the dead and casting out demons to validate that He is who He says He is. Jesus is still appearing in dreams and visions to people as He calls them to Himself.

Out of the 50 church planters, at least 20 of them had come to faith in Jesus because He had appeared to them in a dream.

One brother recalled seeing Jesus standing in the midst of a bright light which illuminated the entire room. Jesus was calling to him, proclaiming himself to be the Son of God. This brother said he fully surrendered and began to share his experience with his family and friends.

One of the ladies said that she and her husband lived

with his family, which is not unusual in this part of the world. Her mother-in-law had been possessed by a demon, which spewed venomous words to anyone who would try to interact with her. No one in the family was a believer in Jesus. As they watched what was taking place, Satan continued to tear down this family, trying day by day to destroy them.

Occasionally, there would be "holy men" that would come through the village. When they came close, the demon would hiss, yell, and spit. One day, a church planter with Biglife came into the house, preaching the word and confronting the demon in the name of Jesus.

He walked over, and as the family watched, he slid his Bible under the pillow of the demon-possessed woman. The next morning, the woman was in her right mind. Just the proximity of the Word of God caused the demon to flee. The church planter shared the gospel and the entire family came to faith in Jesus. This woman and her husband are now planting churches all across Nepal.

God is still at work among those who have never heard the name of Jesus. He is working miracles to show His power and to call those who do not know Him to come to faith. It is a reminder that the same God who performed signs and wonders in the first century is still using them today.

Arash's Story

• • •

In February of 2017, Josh Clarke (who was at that time, the Vice President of Development for Doulos) and I had the chance to join our partner, Biglife for their annual celebration. At the event, we had the unique opportunity to be a part of a Skype call with three of the church planters in Afghanistan. Because it was 5:00 a.m. their time, it was not yet daylight, which was a help in keeping them safe during our conversation. In countries like this, it is often necessary to do Kingdom work under the cover of darkness. The man in the middle had a joy on his face that commanded attention. His name was Arash (AH-rash).

Throughout the country, Islamic extremism is attempting to wipe out Christianity. In fact, the last official Christian church in Afghanistan was closed in 2010. Being a former Al Qaeda operative, Arash knew this better than most. He was taught how to promote Islam with others, and if they rejected it, to eliminate them. He believed that killing infidels was the only way to please Allah and have a chance at getting to heaven.

However, the more he fought, the more he questioned what he was doing. He became depressed and longed to die in jihad. Then one day, his life was radically changed. He had a dream in which he saw Jesus standing in the middle of a room.

Jesus was talking to a group of people, and Arash asked Him a question. He said, "Jesus, some people say that you died and that now you are alive. Tell me Jesus, what really happened." Jesus replied, "Come to me. I want to change your ways." Arash said he kneeled before Jesus asking forgiveness for what he had done and gave his life to Him.

Arash began to study the Bible. He said, "My attitude and the way I treated my wife and children changed. I began to see how Jesus was about giving life and not taking life. God is not a God of hate, but a God of love."

He grew in leaps and bounds and continued studying the Bible, learning what it meant to be a fully devoted follower of Jesus. He has a passion to reach his fellow Afghans for Christ.

He shared with us about what was going on with the ministry in Afghanistan, how the gospel was spreading throughout the country and the need for Bibles in their language. He talked about the persecution that was happening and pleaded for prayer coverage. Then, Arash shared a story of his own.

One day, he was attacked because of his belief in Jesus. He was beaten almost to the point of death. As he laid there bleeding, a man came by and helped him get to the hospital. The doctors were finally able to close the wound and he recovered.

He said, "They might kill me, but God's work will never stop." Where he once trained other Al Qaeda operatives, now he trains others to evangelize and disciple new believers.

You see, converted Muslims don't see other Muslims as the enemy, they see them as brothers who have not yet heard and received the truth. Here is a man who walks in danger every day and yet is unafraid of being found and killed for the gospel. May we live our lives with the same kind of courage and commitment.

David and
Board Member,
Tofey Leon,
with a local
church planter
in the state of
Punjab.

Klem, while
hosting the
Doulos team in
Cambodia. You
can find Klem's
story featured
on page 93.

Gregg Morrison,
Lev Bragg and
David coming
down the
mountain from
sharing the gospel
with a new church
plant in India.

Board member, Rusty Hicks (left), and Executive Director of Biglife, John Heerema (right), discussing ministry strategy while visiting the Middle East.

Deiu Sanh and his wife, Thi Nhem, visiting with the Doulos team in Cambodia. Their story is featured on page 86.

David with Bittu and his father on a trip to India. Bittu's story is featured on page 90.

CHAPTER 8
Reaching Souls: Expansion into Africa

Our third ministry partner is Reaching Souls. The Lord worked through me, this time, to bring this partnership together. It was not the way we had it planned, but it was really cool the way that God worked it out. Let me share a little of the story.

The initial call from the Lord to expand to the continent of Africa came to me in late 2009. We were just a year old in our partnership with World Link in Cuba and had just started our work with Biglife in Central and Southeast Asia. In a quiet time, as I was praying for our men and women in the field, the Lord gave me a vision to be a part of His movement on the continent of Africa. I kept it to myself because I wasn't sure what to say to anyone on our team about the next steps.

However, I held the vision the Lord had given at the forefront of my mind and consistently made it a part of my prayers. Africa was now planted firmly in my heart. Just as He had before, I was asking the Lord to supernaturally bring about a third partner.

In November of 2010, I received a phone call from Manny Fernandez about our upcoming trip to Cuba. He asked if I would consider letting us add one more person to the group going in February. He had a request from a man from Oklahoma that was interested in seeing the work. My first thought was negative. Our trips to the field have a two-fold purpose; we go to see and vet the ongoing work, and we go to show our donors a snapshot of what is being done. The teams are kept small so that we can be flexible and mobile. I was unsure of how adding another person, not one of our team, would impact the dynamics of the trip. Before I could answer, the Holy Spirit moved and it was clear that my response was to be YES.

The months passed and it was time for us to leave for the trip. We landed in Havana, got off the plane and loaded into the van, just as we had on many trips before. I made my way to the back and introduced myself to the team member I did not know. His name was Brent Parsons.

I asked Brent about his reason for coming. He explained that the ministry he worked for was considering expanding their efforts into Cuba. They wanted a closer look at the work on the ground before making a final decision. I wanted to know more about the ministry, where they were currently involved and the methods that they used. For the very first time, I heard about Reaching Souls International and their work in seven countries in East Africa. He told me they only used indigenous leaders. Bells and whistles were going off in my head like crazy. I could feel the presence of the Holy Spirit. For over a year, I had been praying and proceeding, waiting for the Lord to move on bringing us a partner to work with in Africa. It was there, in Havana, that He had done just that.

We spent the week working alongside our church planters on the ground in Cuba as we normally do. We had the chance to preach, teach, baptize and provide some training opportunities for the leaders. But with every free minute, Brent and I were talking about the work taking place in Africa. At the end of our time in Cuba, we parted ways, but I knew our journey had just begun.

Upon landing in the United States, I picked up my phone and immediately called our Chairman of the Board, Thomas Minor. Expecting to hear about the trip to Cuba, Thomas was surprised to learn that I felt that the Lord had shown me a possible new partner to begin work in Africa. After walking through the details of the ministry and all that I had heard over the week, Thomas agreed that our next step should be for the two of us to fly to their office in Oklahoma City and see what the Lord might have in store.

We spent an entire day with the staff of Reaching Souls learning about their history and the current work taking place. We shared our call to partner with established ministries that were empowering indigenous church planters for evangelism, discipleship and church planting. They walked us through the details of training the workers and the financial support that was given to those hired. It was clear with every aspect of the conversation that the vision and mission of our two organizations were completely in sync.

After returning to Birmingham, Thomas and I informed the Board of Directors of what had taken place and how we felt the Lord was telling us to proceed. To continue the vetting process, Brent and I coordinated schedules and planned a trip for me to be on the field with him in Malawi to see the work firsthand.

I was excited about Reaching Souls, and that only increased as I set foot in Africa. The idea of partnering with them was totally affirmed as I served alongside the indigenous leaders and saw the fruit.

The church planters made their way into villages on bicycles with portable sound systems strapped on the back, singing at the top of their lungs. It was awesome to see the way the people in the village gathered around to hear what they had to say. They preached with intensity, the message was clear, and the doctrine was sound. It was a beautiful picture of a first century-type movement. People were coming to faith in Christ, discipleship was taking place, and churches were being planted.

> **They preached with intensity, the message was clear, and the doctrine was sound.**

At our next board meeting, I reported that after discussions with the domestic team in their home office in Oklahoma and then traveling to see the work in action, Thomas and I felt like the Lord had provided a third partner. With their approval, we would begin work with Reaching Souls and expand the work into Africa. All we needed now was the money.

In June of 2011, God gave us an unexpected $3,000 a month and we knew exactly what it was for. We used that to begin our support to Africa. By 2017, our average monthly investment had grown to $18,250.

As of April 2018, we have put almost $900,000 into 10 countries spanning the African continent. As our President, Josh Clarke, would say, "Look at the Lord!"

It is incredible to see what the Lord has done beginning in the back of a van in Havana, Cuba. One of the greatest joys of my life is to see the hand of God at work. This partnership, as with World Link and Biglife, is one that was truly made in heaven.

CHAPTER 9
Africa: The Stories of the Faithful

These are the countries of "low hanging fruit." This doesn't mean the work is easy. However, the receptivity is high, and Africa is open to the gospel at this time.

Our indigenous pastors there say, "Everywhere is a pulpit!" These men and women are making the most of every opportunity to bring in the harvest. The following pages bear witness to those who are advancing the Kingdom. My prayer is that these stories will both convict you and inspire you, as they do me.

Charles' Story

• • •

On that first trip to Malawi, Africa, I met Charles Changala (Chen-gahla), the Associate National Director overseeing the work in Malawi, Zambia and Zimbabwe. At that time, he had been in that position for about five years. Charles, more than anyone I have met in the field, is the perfect example of humble servant leadership. He is a very quiet man, but he is a great leader, pastor, and evangelist.

Charles grew up in a Christian home. His mother and father were believers and took him to church beginning at an early age. Charles sang in the choir and rarely missed a Sunday, but by his confession, he was not a believer. He said that going to church and doing these activities were used as seeds that God had cast into his life, but they were not taking root.

In September of 1993, his father passed away. After the funeral, the pastor came to their home to minister to their family. Charles was 21 years old. The pastor asked him a serious question: "Are you confident that if you were to die today, you would go to heaven?"

Charles' immediate answer was yes, but as the pastor continued to walk through the scriptures, the Holy Spirit revealed to him that he was not a Christian.

He realized that he had a head knowledge from his attendance in church but not a heart knowledge, and he had no relationship with Jesus.

With the pastor at his side, Charles came to Jesus by grace through faith. Charles fully surrendered to Jesus and asked him to take control of his life. As he grew in his faith, Charles became bold and told everyone he talked to about what Jesus had done in his life. Over time, he began to recognize that God was placing in him a passion to preach, teach, and minister to people.

In 1998, Charles went to Bible College and then went on to seminary. After graduating, he was called to pastor the church of his childhood, Mphapa (um-FA-pa) Baptist Church. In 2002, two years later, Reaching Souls came to Mangochi (Man-GO-key) to do a Leadership Development Institute (LDI).

Let me help you understand this unique strategy developed by Reaching Souls. This program gives the indigenous church planters practical and theological training. It is the heartbeat of the work in Africa.

The LDI consists of 250 indigenous church planters and 50 of their wives that are vetted and invited to gather together for a four-day training. During that time, 20 classes are taught, covering the topics of:

How To Study The Bible	Doctrine of The Bible	Doctrine of God
Doctrine of Christ	Doctrine of the Church	Doctrine of the Holy Spirit
Doctrine of Creation	Doctrine of Salvation	Doctrine of Last Things
Personal Devotion	Stewardship	Assurance of Eternal Life
Personal Testimony	Using the EvangeCube	Christian Leadership
Marriage	Pastoral Priorities	Care of a New Christian
Giving an Invitation	Evangelizing Muslims	Preeminence
Worship	Forgiveness	Lifestyle Evangelism
Eternal Rewards	Spiritual Warfare	Relying on the Holy Spirit

The church planters are divided up into groups of 50 and rotate classrooms throughout the day. The first night, everyone gathers in a room for a worship service. Every church planter is presented a complete Bible in their language. For many of them, it is the very first time they have ever received God's word in its entirety.

As they receive them, the church planters weep, jump, sing, shout, and bang on drums. They are overwhelmed with joy to have a full copy of the Word of God that they can read in their native tongue. (It is quite humbling, considering how much we take having multiple copies of the Word in our homes for granted.)

After four days of classroom training, the church planters and the U.S. team of teachers are divided into groups. They then go into the cities, towns and villages to put into practice all that was learned. There are both one-on-one and open-air meetings. The first day, the U.S. team of teachers lead the gatherings and model what has been taught. The next two days, the church planters lead and the U.S. team watch and evaluate.

As decisions for Christ are made, the church planters collect information and location of homes. The new believer is given a form to fill out and told when and where the nearest church will be meeting, and asked to bring it with them. They are promised a gift of the New Testament in their language. The church planter is now responsible for connecting with these new believers and discipling them. It is not unusual for there to be thousands reached in this three-day period.

It is important to note here that only a portion of these indigenous leaders will be chosen to be hired and supported financially by Reaching Souls as they have the funds committed. Many, if not most, of those trained will continue to work a secular job, doing their ministry part-time until funding becomes available.

It was through this LDI training and development that God opened a door for Charles to understand the multiplication and replication of the gospel. He now had a plan and practical way to move forward. He also received a complete copy of the Bible for the first time in his life.

In February 2003, Charles was hired by Reaching Souls, giving him monthly financial support and providing him with a community for encouragement. They also supplied the tools that would make his ministry more effective and efficient.

Charles has been a part of leading over 50,000 people to faith in Christ, while planting 18 churches in the villages around him. Charles' story is all too familiar. I believe that there are many people worldwide who have a head knowledge of Jesus but not a relationship with Him. I pray that this is not your story as well.

Can you answer with complete confidence that if you were to die today that you would spend eternity in heaven? If you cannot, please do what Charles did and talk to someone who can walk you through that decision. Not only will that secure your eternal destination, it will also launch you into opportunities to make Jesus' name known.

Samuel's Story

• • •

While in Malawi, Africa, in the spring of 2011, I had the chance to get to know the National Director of the country, Samuel Mwale (Mwah-lee).

Samuel was born into a home where his parents were Jehovah's Witnesses and was brought up in that tradition. As he got older, Samuel became a missionary or witness for the church. However, the more he communicated the doctrine and theology to others, the more questions he had.

In 1975, the Leadership of Jehovah's Witnesses proclaimed that the world would be coming to an end. When it didn't, Samuel was left with more questions and many doubts. He moved away from his parents and began searching for the truth. He poured over the scriptures and visited other churches to hear their doctrine and theology.

One night at a revival, Samuel heard the gospel preached and it lined up with all he had been studying. Samuel understood that he was the sinner for whom Jesus died. Before leaving the service that night, Samuel had placed his faith in Christ.

After his conversion, he joined a new church plant in the area where he was living. Within two years, Samuel helped plant two new churches and he felt the call on his life to become a church planter/national missionary. He enrolled in a two-year Bible school in Lilongwe (le-LONG-weh), the capital city of Malawi. Upon completion, he moved to Zimbabwe to finish a four-year program in theological training.

When he came home during breaks, Samuel would tell his parents about his studies and share the gospel with them. He smiled as he reported to us that his mom came to faith in Christ first, and then shortly after, his father believed. After his four-year program, he was called as Associate Pastor for The Capital City Baptist Church in Lilongwe.

It was while he was there that he heard about Reaching Souls. He was invited to be a part of an LDI. While attending, the Lord gave him a clear mission. He wanted Samuel to go back to his hometown, share the gospel, and plant churches. Many pastors were moving from the rural areas into the cities, but the Lord was calling him to go from the city back to the rural areas. Isn't it so like God to do what seems to us to be counter-productive?

Nervously, he told his wife and, much to his surprise, she felt the exact same call. It is so powerful for me to watch God call someone to ministry and speak simultaneously to their mate. (That is certainly mine and Susan's testimony.) He went to his church to let them know his plans, and again Samuel was surprised. They wanted to be a part of sending them back to his hometown and pledged their prayer and financial support. They helped renovate a home, install electricity (which is a big, big, deal in Africa), and committed to monetarily supporting them for three years. (Wow, that is so similar to our story with MG&A.) Samuel stood in awe of the Lord's provision.

After three years, he was recruited by Reaching Souls to become a national missionary. In 2000, Samuel was named an Associate National Director, and in 2003, he was named the National Director of Malawi. His team has been a part of planting over 50 churches across the country. The Lord has allowed Samuel to be a part of seeing over 105,000 professions of faith.

One of my last days in the country, we were staying in a game reserve compound. We had been instructed to be careful going out by ourselves after dark because bull elephants had recently been seen in the area. Very early that morning as the sun was just rising, I stepped out of my tent and looked towards the water to see a silhouette of a man on his knees praying. There, praying for the souls of his country, was Samuel Mwale. My prayer, that day and every day, is that I will be that committed to reach my country and to carry out the Great Commission with that kind of passion.

Fraywell's Story

• • •

Fraywell (Fry-well) Chipeta (Cha-payta), the Southern Director for Africa, is a strong physical man, and yet, a gentle giant. On our first official trip to Africa with Reaching Souls as a partner, we went to Lusaka, Zambia, Fraywell's hometown. I was so excited to have the opportunity to get to know this man in a deeper way as I served alongside of him in his city and at his church. We worshipped with him and his congregation and helped baptize over 100 people in the service that day.

Fraywell is the oldest of two boys. His early childhood home was a happy one. However, when he was ten years old, his father took a second wife, which is not uncommon in that culture. From that moment forward, his home life changed drastically.

There was so much friction and resentment between his father and mother and between his mother and the second wife. Alcohol and drunkenness became a way of life in his home. Every evening brought more fighting and bickering. He grew to hate his father as he watched him drink and beat his mother on a daily basis. He ran away from home and became a "street kid" in Lusaka. He became a part of a street gang that gave him a sense of belonging. He saw it as his only choice for protection and resources. They would beat people to steal from them. They were criminals and their names and faces hung on wanted posters.

One day, they beat and robbed a man who was able to

get up and go straight to the police. He identified the gang and instructed the officers on where to find them. The confrontation turned violent and the police opened fire. Five of the men that were with Fraywell were shot dead in the street. Only Fraywell made it out alive. To this day, he pauses as he tells the story and reminds us that he cannot describe how he escaped. At the age of 14, he was again homeless and now on the run.

He had a childhood friend with whom he still had contact, and he turned to him for help. The friend had one condition for Fraywell to be able to stay with him; he must go to church. You see, this friend was a Christian and knew that Fraywell needed Jesus more than anything else in his life. Fraywell was reluctant, fearing discovery by the authorities, but he seemingly had no other option. He agreed. The third week he attended the church, an evangelistic team from Texas had come to preach. The text was from Romans Chapter 5. Fraywell realized that he was a sinner in need of Jesus for salvation. On that day, as a teenager who had been through so much, he gave his life to Jesus.

Fraywell later heard the Lord calling him into full-time ministry. After his completion of Bible School training, he was asked to serve as pastor of Garden Central Baptist Church. He had a deep desire to see his congregation grow and tried everything he knew to make that happen. He would put up posters and host revivals and no one would come. Then, one day, he was invited to participate in an LDI with Reaching Souls.

This gave him the skills he needed to take his theological education into the streets and reach the people in his community. He went into the marketplace after services and throughout the week. He shared the gospel one on one and did open-air preaching. He would then invite all those who had heard the message to attend services the next Sunday. The church was soon bursting at the seams with new believers.

To date, Fraywell has planted 23 new churches and mentored 16 evangelists. He has employed 6 full-time pastors to oversee the church plants and hired 2 assistant pastors to help with the work at Garden Central. He continues to faithfully serve the Lord with a deep commitment to open-air meetings, developing new leaders and planting new churches. I could sit with Fraywell all day and share about the things of the Lord. As we say in America, "He is the real deal."

Paul's Story

• • •

In June of 2013, it was my first time to be in the country of Zimbabwe. At an LDI event, I had the pleasure of meeting Paul Karani (kah-RAH-nee). In stature, he is a small man, but a giant for the Kingdom of God. He is such a servant-leader, as so many of the men that we serve with all over the world are. When he comes into a room, he has the ability to assume a leadership role without even opening his mouth. He does this by meeting people where they are and serving them well. In turn, people willingly follow his leadership. He truly works as unto the Lord.

Paul was born into a pagan family, but when he was four years old, that all changed. His parents heard the gospel proclaimed and placed their trust in Jesus. They started attending church, which meant that Paul did as well.

As Paul grew, so did his leadership responsibilities at church. He became a Sunday School teacher and then was asked to help lead the choir. There was one problem: Paul wasn't a Christian.

Later in his teenage years, his church planned an evangelistic crusade for their community. Paul was on hand, as always, to help set up and invite others to come.

The crusade began and Paul was in his place. While he had heard the gospel proclaimed many times before, this night was different. The pastor began his sermon by declaring the Biblical truth that salvation did not come through the heritage of friends or parents. He explained that salvation could not be passed down to you from someone else. His challenge to those in attendance was for each person to stand and give an account before the Lord of their own personal salvation. Paul realized that he had no such story. He was living on the experiences of his family. Paul Karani knew then that he was lost and was in need of a Savior. Paul recalls that it was in that moment that Jesus saved him and began to transform his life.

He continued to faithfully serve the church. He went to college, graduated and taught in a government school for 18 years. However, he was miserable. Paul knew in his heart that the Lord had called him into ministry, but he was running from that call. Then a series of strange things began to happen.

Month after month, different events would conspire to consume his paycheck. Sick children, multiple doctor visits, medicines to buy. By the time he would make it home from picking up his paycheck, it would be spent.

Paul had taken out a loan to start a retail business, but with all of the health problems of his family, his business never got off the ground. He was perplexed at the events in his life, so he went before the Lord asking Him what was happening. Very clearly, the Lord reminded Paul of the call that was placed on his life for ministry and because of his unwillingness to yield, the Lord told him that He had been trying to get his attention. He immediately went and resigned his position from the school. As he walked home that day, he was empty-handed and fully trusting that the Lord had a plan for the days ahead.

Six months passed and Paul still had no job. It was a

difficult time, as you can imagine, trying to take care of his wife and children with no income. Even still, Paul continued to be faithful in his peaching and teaching of the Word. One day, he met a man who was serving as the National Director of Kenya for Reaching Souls. He extended an invitation for Paul to have an interview to become a church planter/national missionary.

It did not take long to see that he had the gift of leadership. Soon after, he was asked to serve as the Associate National Director for Kenya, helping oversee the work taking place across the country.

In 2007, Reaching Souls elevated Paul to the position of Associate Director for East Africa, where he helped oversee the work in six countries.

But the Lord wasn't finished yet. In 2015, Paul was placed at the top of the leadership team as he became the East Africa Director. At the time of this writing, he currently provides oversight for the 1,065 national missionaries in that area.

The Lord took a man running from the call on his life and placed him into a major leadership role. Isn't that just like Jesus? He has allowed Paul to be a part of planting 40 churches and seeing over 50,000 people make professions of faith in Christ since he started with Reaching Souls.

Huessein's Story

• • •

In the summer of 2014, I made a trip with Reaching Souls to participate in the LDI as a part of the new work taking place in Burundi. It was being held right outside of the capital city of Bujumbura (boo-jum-BOOR-ah), and where I first met Hussein (hoo-SANE) Abdi (aab-Dee). When he received his copy of the Bible, he shouted at the top of his lungs and he jumped and danced before the Lord with great excitement. It was the most uninhibited worship and joy that I had ever experienced.

Hussein had come to the LDI in Burundi from the country of Kenya. After dinner one evening, we had the opportunity to sit with Hussein and hear about how the Lord had changed his life.

Hussein had been raised in a very strict Muslim family. As he continued to grow, he had been singled out as a leader in his mosque and would rise early every morning to be a part of the call to prayer. One morning in 2009, when he was on the way to the mosque for the call to prayer Hussein lost his voice. He literally became mute. His voice had been taken away and he was unable to participate. He was distraught and confused by what was happening, so he went out into the city and started wandering the streets.

Reaching Souls was holding an LDI in Kenya and had deployed the church planters into the streets for their practical training. Hussein met one of these church planters and listened as he began to share the gospel with him. It was there in the streets of the city that he heard about Jesus for the first time. Hussein made his profession of faith in Christ and rejected all that he had once believed as a lie.

He joined the church planters at the open-air meeting and made his decision public. Elias (AA-lee-us) Kashambagani (CAASH-um-bah-GAAN-ee), one of the church leaders, met with Hussein and challenged him to go home and tell his family that he was now following Christ. His voice now restored, he did as instructed. He went home, and as he walked in the door, he was confronted by his father. He had already heard of Hussein's conversion and asked if it was true. Without hesitation, Hussein said that he had heard the truth of the gospel and fully believed that Jesus Christ was the Son of the One, true living God. He was now forgiven and reconciled to God through Christ. His father demanded that he leave their house.

As with many Muslim families around the world, when a person comes to faith in Christ, they are disowned by their family. Hussein returned later that day to collect his belongings. When he arrived, his sister told him that their father had burned everything with the exception of one pair of clothes that she had hidden for him. The next morning, Hussein went to the church close to where the LDI was being held. During the service, he was invited to come down and share his testimony.

Hussein proclaimed the name of Jesus and how he brought him from death to life. That afternoon, he was called on again to give his testimony at an open-air meeting that was taking place. Within 24 hours, Hussein was telling anyone and everyone who would listen about Jesus.

Hussein went on to be discipled and trained for the work of a church planter with Reaching Souls in 2011. In 2017, I had the chance to reconnect with Hussein and hear how the Lord had been using him. He and his wife have been sharing the gospel among the Muslim population in Kenya. He has been a part of seeing over 33,000 professions of faith and has helped plant six churches. To God be the glory!

David's Story

• • •

In February of 2017, I met David Okecho (O-Ke-chO) for the first time. He had come to the United States with Reaching Souls to visit with some of their supporters and he and Brent Parsons made their way to the Doulos Partners office to spend some time with us. Susan and I enjoyed getting to host them in our home, and we especially enjoyed the time we had to hear David's story.

David was born in the village of Butamira, near Jinja, Uganda. He was raised in a pagan family and alcohol addiction was prevalent. His parents died when he was young. With the absence of knowledge of the Lord and the death of his parents, David lacked a moral compass or a firm foundation. Even the name of the village told a story: Butamira means "the place of the drunkard."

Growing up, David didn't go to school and never learned to read or write. However, he was gifted with an ear for the English language. In 1982, there was a preacher that came to their village. From the pulpit, he talked about John 3:16. It was the first time in David's life that he realized that there was a God that loved him and wanted a relationship with him. In fact, God sent His son to die so that could be possible. In that service, when the invitation was given, David and his wife, Margaret, stood up and gave their lives Christ.

The depth of forgiveness that he felt was profound. His life was a mess. His marriage to Margaret was an arranged one based on paganism. His love of alcohol was evident.

However, that day, he felt that he was truly transformed. He stopped drinking and made his marriage with Margaret right before the Lord. From 1982 to 1996, he continued to grow in his faith and became active in his church to learn how to walk out his salvation. In 1996, God called David to serve Him full-time. He wasn't sure exactly what that meant, but knew that he was supposed to be sharing the gospel and gathering believers together so that they could grow. There in his hometown of Butamira, David started Musisi Grace Baptist Church.

He chose the name so that the town would know that, by God's grace, He can change even those who are drunkards. They began to see people go from being negatively affected by alcohol to positively changed by God. They shared the gospel any chance they had and saw people coming to know the Lord. Before they knew it, they had begun 50 daughter churches in the surrounding area.

Two years later, David's friend, Tabu, told him about how Reaching Souls was interviewing pastors who could join them in working across the country as evangelists and church planters. David questioned his ability to even fill out the application because of his illiteracy, but the Holy Spirit affirmed in him to move forward and meet with the ministry.

The team was interviewing 40 pastors from the area but many questioned David's ability to be hired because he couldn't read or write. However, David was one of the 20 church planters selected to begin work in Uganda.

After some time, David became the Associate National Director, then later the National Director, overseeing all of the work in Uganda. Under his leadership, they have grown from 34 missionaries to 100 missionaries and he has been able to be a part of seeing 45,000 people come to faith in Christ through his immediate ministry.

David Okecho not only was in our home in February of 2017, but he welcomed Susan and me into his home when we took a team to Uganda in the summer of that same year. Josh Clarke, who was with us, had the opportunity to preach in the very church that David had started in Butamira. We had the honor of baptizing new believers in a river near the town. We traveled with him from village to village and met those church planters who are on the front lines of the Kingdom work taking place in Uganda.

We were also able to be a part of the housewarming party for the Okecho family as they opened and dedicated their new home to the Lord.

The entire village turned out to celebrate. The Okecho family along with the brothers and sisters from the church, fed everyone who came. I also had the incredible opportunity to preach the gospel at this event. By the way, when was the last time you went to that kind of party and had a gospel message preached? We prayed a prayer of blessing not only over the new house, but over the work that David and his church planters are doing in the country of Uganda. This was truly one of the highlights of things that I have done while in the field.

128

Hussein Abdi and his family at their home in Kenya. His story is featured on page 121.

Fraywell Chipeta (second from right) with David and Josh at the home of John Wright, sharing what God is doing in Zambia.

Samuel Mwale praying for the people of Malawi at dawn. His story can be found on page 112.

David, Susan and Josh visiting a local church planter and his family in Uganda.

A local church planter, Julius, sharing the gospel using the Evangecube in the streets of Burundi.

Support of local church planters in Africa include a bicycle. Here are a group of them on their bikes ready to go out and share the gospel.

SECTION 3

To the Ends of the Earth:
The Next 10 Years

CHAPTER 10
A Growing Team

In the early days of Doulos Partners, our team was small. In addition to Wayne, Scott and our first couple of board members, the Lord placed some incredibly gifted people around me to help move the ministry forward, some of which were my family. God had not only been preparing me but also my wife of 42 years, Susan, our son, Brian, and our daughter, Bethany, to answer His call and to become some of the first workers in the ministry.

I knew that Susan would be an invaluable piece to what God was calling us to be a part of, as she had throughout our life together. However, I could have never imagined all that the Lord would use her to do as part of the Doulos team. As a retired member of the financial services industry, she immediately volunteered to take on the entirety of the back-office support. Susan stepped up to the challenge as we began to think about financial accountability, payment processing, and donor reporting.

She pulled from her work experience and was able to problem-solve a number of areas that helped us get moving in a positive direction. Because of her training and spiritual gifts, along with support from our Board of Directors, the processes she put into place helped us in achieving our accreditation with the Evangelical Council of Financial Accountability (ECFA). This organization grants accreditation to nonprofits which have sound financial procedures in place. Susan has also been responsible for our tax reporting to the IRS and for financial reporting to our Board of Directors. She handles everything from payroll and taxes to ensuring every donation is accounted for in our systems.

Two years after our founding, Brian came on our staff to help ensure that the growing technology needs of the ministry would be met; a position he still holds today part-time. He has continued to help develop a robust platform for us to engage our donors and partners around the globe. Brian has helped create an environment for our growing team with all aspects of technological support. He has also gone with us to the field twice to see the work and capture video and still images that have helped us tell the stories of the men and women on the front lines in the most compelling way possible.

There are many ways that Bethany has been a part of Doulos over the years. With a background in communications, she has the skill set that allowed her to help create copy to convey what God is doing in venues like our website and mail-outs. She has such a keen eye for things like how to tell a story through visual mediums.

Early on, I knew we needed a logo for the ministry but this was definitely out of my area of expertise. I immediately called on her to help to assist us in designing a graphic that would visually help identify what God was doing in and through Doulos Partners.

In the beginning, there were just a few of us having the conversations and dreaming the dreams that would lead to the start-up of Doulos Partners. As small as it was, we were the team. Since then, the Lord has assembled great leaders and has brought many new people to get the mission accomplished.

I can't say enough about our Board of Directors. I have served on many boards over the years, but this is the most efficient and effective that I have ever seen. Lev Bragg, our earliest Board Member, Thomas Minor, our Chairman, and that entire team have such a strong desire to see the name of Jesus go forward. Each member loves the Lord and is committed to not only financially support the ministry, but to prayerfully intercede on its behalf and for the men and women in the field. At the time of this writing there are 16 Board Members that are serving Doulos with their yes on the table. They are saying yes to faithful stewardship and to active involvement in the Great Commission.

> **I have served on many boards over the years, but this is the most efficient and effective that I have ever seen.**

I am also deeply indebted to our partners around the globe. These ministries had already said yes to empowering indigenous leaders to reach their nation with the gospel before Doulos was even an idea. We began with one partner in one country. Now there are three partners that span 36 countries on 4 different continents. They are made up of 7,000 to 8,000 national missionaries/church planters that are being supported by Doulos Partners. And we certainly cannot omit the incredible domestic teams that run their home offices from here in the United States.

The most humbling area of growth comes from those who have become donors. Because of the commitment of our Board of Directors to cover all of the administrative costs, 100% of all the money that has been given by our donors has gone straight to the field to support a church planter and their family. As we share the vision, tell the story, and ask people to get involved, the Lord continues to bring donors from all over the US to support these indigenous missionaries. At the time of this writing, we have almost 400 people who are following the Lord's prompting and saying yes to finically supporting the work of Doulos Partners. This group has given over 6,800 times, which has allowed us to send over $3.5 million dollars, through our partners, to the field.

One of the greatest areas of interest for both our staff and our board has been that of succession. If Doulos Partners was to continue on, who would the Lord allow to lead it into the next chapter?

As I was getting older and the ministry continued to grow, we had a deep desire and need to reach the next generation of donors and leaders. We began to look for specific ways that we could mentor those who could advance the gospel both through Doulos and their local churches.

May 20, 2016, will be a day that I will not soon forget. As I was having breakfast with Lev Bragg, we were spending time in prayer for our families and each other's children. He asked me to pray for his oldest daughter, Courtney, and her husband, Josh. Lev began to share about Josh's professional career in development in higher education, his leadership in churches as a pastor, and the heart of both Josh and Courtney for the nations. Josh was finishing up his doctorate and would be defending his dissertation on fundraising that summer, and he felt like God was opening up a new season of service for them. The Holy Spirit very clearly said to me that Josh was a man that I needed to talk to.

Later that afternoon, I had an hour-long conversation with him. We both knew that God was at work. Our leadership went through the process of spending time with both Josh and Courtney, we all knew that this was the right next step for both Doulos and the Clarke family.

On July 18, 2016, Josh joined our staff as the Vice President of Development. It was apparent to me then, but even more today, that God brought Josh and Courtney Clarke along with their four children to not only be a part of Doulos Partners now, but to play a strategic and integral role in the future of the ministry. This was affirmed again by the work of the Holy Spirit and the recommendation of our Board of Directors as Josh was named President of Doulos Partners in March of 2018. This young man is both called and capable to serve the Lord, Doulos Partners, and the next generation of the

Doulos Team.

I would be remiss if I didn't take a moment to mention our team of volunteers that give tirelessly of themselves. Marcia Lowry, Amanda Myrick, and my wife, Susan, all donate endless hours in our back office. Wallis Haynes spends much of his time to keep our donors informed of the many prayer needs of our men and women in the field. We, at Doulos, are so thankful for our volunteers. It is truly a joy to serve with them.

There is a ripening harvest and we are called to be as prepared as we can be for the work that is ahead. In 2017, Thomas Minor, Kevin Halcomb, one of the newest members of our board, and Josh Clarke, brought up the idea of a Junior Board in one of our full board meetings. Everyone was very excited about this next step of growing our team. It would give us an opportunity to engage and equip the next generation of leaders for both Doulos and Christendom.

This Junior Board, with an average age of 27, consists of individuals who are already investing in Doulos, have a deep desire to see people won for Christ, and have been on the field with us to see the work with their own eyes.

These young leaders and their families want to be a part of something that is about "storing up treasures in heaven rather than on earth." There is great excitement as the Lord has brought together this group to help provide advice and direction as we continue to advance the call that God gave us from day one.

The fields truly are white unto harvest. God has clearly gathered an incredible group of people together at Doulos from our Board of Directors, to the Junior Board, to the staff, to our donors, to the partners in the field, for the single purpose of making the name of Jesus known. I am more excited than I have ever been about the future of Doulos Partners as we continue to celebrate the people that the Lord is sending to carry out His Great Commission both now and in the years to come.

CHAPTER 11
A Ripening Harvest

I am constantly reminded about how quickly things change around us.

Each time that I visit the World Population Clock website and watch the number of people in the world move in real time, I see the need to stay focused on what the Lord has called us to do.

As I meet with people, I often encourage them to spend some time on that site to see the speed at which the population in our world is changing. By doing the math you can see that every second almost five people are born and two people die. That leads to an annual net population growth of around 80 to 90 million people.

Out of a world population of 7.6 billion people, it is estimated that there are around three billion who have never heard the name of Jesus. That's about 40%. According to the population clock, two people die every second, or about 175,000 per day. 40% of 175,000 (70,000) are dying daily without ever having an opportunity to hear the gospel.

At the forefront of our minds at Doulos is always the question, "What's the best way to reach the unreached?" In light of this fact, our team at Doulos is constantly evaluating the countries we invest in that are becoming sustainable (20% of the population considered Christian believers) so that we can move those dollars to areas in less evangelized places. We want to invest our donors' dollars in the most fruitful way.

We also feel it is vitally important to get the money to the field as quickly as we can to deploy as many workers as possible. Holding only enough to cover our first two weeks of administrative costs, we empty our bank account every month, dividing it among our three partners.

We understand that this goes against every earthly sound accounting principal, but in God's economy, it makes perfect sense. Hence, our mission statement: To reach the maximum number of people, in the shortest amount of time, in the most cost-effective way.

There are two specific new areas of work that God has brought to the attention of Doulos Partners in the recent months to address and take advantage of this ripening harvest. The first came through

> **Holding only enough to cover our first two weeks of administrative costs, we empty our bank account every month, dividing it among our three partners.**

a conversation with a board member, Lev Bragg, in May of 2017.

While discussing a variety of topics about the ministry, Lev began to talk with me about the prompting of the Lord to research ways that we could be involved with the refugee crisis around the world. To be honest, while I had been following the refugee crisis in the news, I had given no thought about how that could be a part of what was happening at Doulos.

The longer we talked, the more the Holy Spirit stirred within me a desire to be a part of reaching these people with the gospel. We began to do our research, and we found where the United Nations reported that 1 out of 113 people on the planet is a refugee and that we were living in the worst refugee crises since World War II.

We realized that there were refugees fleeing closed countries, some of which are the hardest to penetrate with the gospel and ending up in countries where we could openly share the love of Christ with them. As Josh Clarke likes to say, "It is as if the Lord is quite literally rearranging the ends of the earth so that we can reach them."

We know that there might only be a short window of time for us to come along side of them during this devastating season of their life, to help provide for their physical needs, and in doing so, share the good news of the gospel with them. As we continued to pray, the Lord made clear to us that if we would train and disciple new believers in refugee camps, if or when they were able to go back to their home countries, they would be taking the gospel with them.

142

To do more investigating, I called John Heerema to ask if Biglife had ever considered working with refugees. His reply caught me off guard; they had just spent three days on a retreat laying out a plan the Lord had given them to work with refugees in five different countries.

Shortly after our phone conversation, some of the Biglife leadership team came to Birmingham for a meeting and we solidified our partnership together for engaging with and working to reach refugees.

Another area that has continued to get more and more of our attention is a desire to see the gospel go forth in the 10-40 Window. That may be a phrase that you have never heard of before, so let me explain. If you take the globe and lay it flat, the 10-40 Window is the part on the map that is between 10 degrees latitude north to 40 degrees latitude north of the equator, stretching across Africa and Asia.

Looking all the way across that area, you will find two

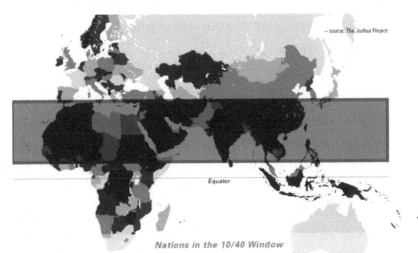

Nations in the 10/40 Window

Afghanistan • Algeria • Bahrain • Bangledesh • Benin • Bhutan • Burkina Faso • Cambodia • Chad China • Cyprus • Djibouti • Egypt • Eritrea • Gambia • Greece • Guinea • Guinea-Bissau • India Iran • Iraq • Israel • Japan • Jordan • Kuwait • Laos • Lebanon • Libya • Mali • Malta • Mauritania Morocco • Myanmar • Nepal • Niger • North Korea • Oman • Pakistan • Philippines • Portugual Qatar • Saudi Arabia • Senegal • South Sudan • Sudan • Syria • Taiwan • Tajikistan • Thailand Tunisia • Turkey • Turkmenistan • United Arab Emirates • Vietnam • Western Sahara • Yemen thirds of the world's population. In regard to mission strategy, only 2% to 3% of the church's mission's dollars go to reach this part of the world. Get this: the smallest percentage of money is invested in one of the largest areas of unreached people groups in the world.

That brings us to the second area of new work. In recent months, we became aware of an organization called the Issachar Initiative. This group plans and executes full day seminars around the country with ministries and business leaders to encourage them to adopt a particular part of the world for the purpose of carrying the gospel to Unengaged, Unreached People Groups (UUPGs).

An Unengaged People Group is a people group that has no Bible in their native tongue, no missionaries present telling the people about Jesus, and no church available for them to attend. An Unreached People Group is one where less than 2% of that group is a professing Christian. In one of our last meetings together with Issachar, their leadership shared that there are approximately 1,150 UUPGs left in the world.

This kind of information is what catches our eye at Doulos. As we began to pray for what the Lord would have us do next or how He would use the men and women in the field that we support, these are the needs that came to mind. We see that there is a ripening harvest and what the Lord is asking for are willing workers to be placed where so many have never heard. After careful vetting and much conversation, our board decided that we needed to engage.

In January of this year (2018), Doulos joined the Issachar Initiative to reach 14 UUPG'S in Cameroon, a country on the coast of west Africa. This is our first step in the Issachar initiative. I have really enjoyed working with Bill Slappey, the owner of Slappey Communications, and Kevin Moore, the Executive Director of Mission Birmingham, who are in charge of overseeing this three-year strategy. This type of collaboration between business leaders, who are providing financial and prayer support, Doulos Partners, who is running point on the initiative, and Biglife who is employing and engaging indigenous leaders who will be taking the gospel forward on the ground, is a beautiful thing to behold. I believe that this is just the way that the Lord intended for us to work together to bring people to Himself.

From my personal experience, the world is becoming less gray. On every issue, especially those theological and spiritual, everything now is more black and white. While some may think that this is a negative place to find ourselves, I see it as a tremendous blessing. It makes it easy for us to see those who are inside and also those who are outside the faith, making our areas to work more defined. Even in the midst of one of the greatest eras of growing persecution and martyrdom in the church around the world, we are seeing the acceleration of a sense of urgency in Christians who want to rapidly make His name known. There is a tenacity, perseverance, and sacrifice because of their understanding of the great need to reach the lost that is constantly before them.

I also cannot help but think of Africa when I think of the ripening harvest. Missions agencies around the world are identifying it as the continent in which there will be the greatest number of new believers in the coming years.

I am excited that Doulos Partners is already at work in 11 countries in Africa, but the work is just beginning.

Around the globe, in both the most fertile soil and the hardest places to reach, there is a ripening harvest. We want to be a part of it all.

We believe that when Jesus told us to go to the ends of the earth, He meant it. When we see the harvest that is before us, we acknowledge that it is a huge task but that with the help of people like yourself under the direction of God's guiding hand, it is a task that can be accomplished.

We, at Doulos, are doing everything in our power to be obedient and unwavering to the call that the Lord has given us, which is to reach the people of this world who do not yet know Jesus.

CHAPTER 12
An Unwavering Obedience

God's call is an amazing thing. It is truly a joy to receive it and to carry it out in our lives. When God compels us to engage, His expectation is for complete obedience and an all-out effort to carry out the task that He has given to be accomplished.

There is something deeply spiritual and sovereign about the call of God on a person's life. We see it throughout Scripture. For example, in Genesis 6 we see God's call on Noah for him to build the ark. God would use a flood to bring His judgment of the sinfulness of mankind and yet the ark was His way of saving Noah and his family, bringing a fresh new start to the earth. Noah was unwavering in his obedience.

I am also reminded of the call of God to Abraham in Genesis Chapter 12, where he was told to leave his homeland to go to a place God had prepared for him and that He was going to make him a great nation. Abraham was unwavering in his obedience.

I think about God's call on Moses in Exodus Chapter 3 that came out of a burning bush that ended up taking Moses back to Egypt to be the instrument God would use to set His people free. Moses was unwavering in his obedience.

I think about God's call on John the Baptist in Matthew Chapter 3 for him to go and preach the message of repentance because the Kingdom of Heaven was at hand. John was unwavering in his obedience.

I think about God's call on the life of Jesus in Luke Chapter 4, to *"proclaim the good news to the poor and to set captives free."* His call, as it says in Luke Chapter 19, was to *"seek and to save that was lost."* Even though Jesus asked God to remove the cup of the death on the cross that was before Him, He told God in an unwavering and powerful response, *"not My will but Yours be done."*

We see the call of God on the life of Paul in Acts Chapter 9, to *"carry My Name before the Gentiles, and kings and the children of Israel."* Paul was unwavering in his obedience.

I believe that every person's response to the call of God should be unwavering and obedient.

Throughout my life, I have watched the lives of other people who have either embraced or rejected the call of God. One that comes to mind is a brother in Christ who, I believe, was set apart to preach. However, due to circumstances and situations, he ran from it and has yet to surrender. I know how hard it is at certain times of life to embrace the assignment God has for us. I ran from my call to ministry for four years. I will always remember that day on April 24,1988, in Savannah, Georgia, walking into the den to tell my wife, Susan, that I could no longer say no to God. Her response was simply to look at me and say, "I know!"

When God speaks, not only is it to the individual person, it is also to their mate if they are married. I know of another man who I believe was being sent to the mission field. To this day, I see that there is a brokenness in him because he was unwilling to accept it and to go to the field. While I cannot know the hearts of these individuals, I can say that the counsel that I gave them was to be obedient to the voice of God because one day we will all stand before the Lord and give an account for what He has asked us to do! I believe there are many calls from God that have been ignored or rejected. I am thankful that in the midst of these, there are many more who have unapologetically and sacrificially answered the Lord with a resounding "yes!"

Since the inception of Doulos Partners, I have been amazed at the number of people who have responded to God's appeal to be a part of what He is doing in and through this ministry. As God turned the first three of us into six, and that six into the thousands that are now involved in the work of Doulos, it has really been interesting to see that there has been an unwavering yes to the call, which is evangelism, discipleship, and church planting. As our board has grown, as the number of partners has grown, as our staff has grown, as the number of our donors has grown, and as our organization has gone through strategic changes, there has been a unity, harmony and sense of urgency about remaining true to empower indigenous leaders to carry out those three things around the world.

I often tell people when I meet with them that when you have a clear directive from the Lord, you have the ability to go through a thought process that clarifies what to say yes to and what to say no to. You are enabled to encourage others in their specific assignments while standing firmly on your own from the Lord.

I am thankful that God has given Doulos Partners a narrow focus. Even as the Lord presents new opportunities for reaching people with the gospel, it stays the same. For example, as we begin to work within the refugee camps, the work of evangelism, discipleship and church planting is being completed by empowering indigenous leaders in the camp. The same is taking place with the work in Cameroon. God is raising up leaders, which are indigenous, to go out in the bush to reach the unengaged and unreached people groups.

As we have grown as an organization, the call of God for us has not changed. Throughout my time in ministry, I have seen many organizations, businesses and ministries that are floundering to complete their mission because they are not focused. They are running after the latest, greatest, most

> With every member of our team, those who have been here from day one and with those who are brand new, we have an unwavering obedience to the Lord.

culturally accepted plan, when all of a sudden, they find themselves a mile wide and an inch deep and totally in the weeds.

I am grateful and humbled to say that God has assembled our team and that by His grace and through His leading we have been able to stay the course. The assignment of evangelism, discipleship and church planting through empowering indigenous leaders in every country and to be on every inhabitable continent has remained unchanged. With every member of our team, those who have been here both from day one and with those who are brand new, we have an unwavering obedience to the Lord.

I hope that commitment is encouraging and comforting to you as a part of the Doulos family. It is very special to be in the center of God's will for our lives. May it ALWAYS be so!

SECTION 4

Your Place in the Story:
Saying Yes

CHAPTER 13
Who Controls Your Yes?

As a little boy, it was obvious who controlled my yes. Especially when I was young, my parents had total control. With my mom, it was a stern look and sometimes "the rod" that helped control my yes. When I was in trouble with my mother, she sent me to pick my own switch from the "switch bush" that was in our backyard. My dad, on the other hand, helped control my yes with his belt. They not only wanted to control my behavior so that we could have some sort of peace in our house, but they did it because they wanted me to be a responsible and respectful young man.

As I began to get older, I realized there were other people in my life who were also trying to control my yes. Classmates, neighbors, teammates, friends, people that I I wanted, or at least I thought I wanted to be my friends, all had a part in my yes. The Lord has created us for right relationships; however, in this fallen world, our desire to be accepted can corrupt us to the point where peer pressure takes hold of our decisions. At times, we allow other people to control our yes. As in my own life, as well as with others, I have found that whoever controls my yes is the one who ultimately controls my actions. For example, if my yes is to be a part of the cool crowd, then I have to act in such a way that the "cool people" will accept me. If I wanted to play in the game, then I had to act in such a way that the coach would put me in to play over someone else on the team.

As I slowly grew in my understanding about the things of God, I realized that Romans 3:23, *"for all have sinned and fall short of the glory of God,"* was talking about me. I understood for the first time that I was sinner and that I could not save myself. The Lord began to reveal to me that the one who was controlling my yes was Satan and that he was the one telling me the lie that I was the ultimate authority over my own life. I realized that I was lost and in need of a Savior.

I am thankful that during that point in my life, a professional baseball played named Al Worthington came to Springhill Baptist Church and preached the gospel. It was because of him walking us through the Roman road that I realized that the one I needed to control my yes was Jesus. That experience showed me that if I was going to have my sins forgiven, it had to start with me saying yes to Him.

Al shared Romans 5:8 which says, *"while we were still sinners, Christ died for us."* He went on to tell about how Jesus led a perfect sinless life and went to the cross and died in our place. It was that night, through the prompting of the Holy Spirit, I "confessed with my mouth and believed in my heart that God had raised Jesus from the dead," said yes to Jesus and was saved.

From that night forward, I have been on a journey to live my life in such a way that Jesus would have complete control over my yes. It doesn't happen every second of every day, but the older I get and the more mature that I become the easier it is to put my total trust in His hands and my yes on the table.

On December 26, 2006, an event in our family changed my life forever. I spoke to my brother, Corey, for the last time. We were having the Johnson family Christmas gathering that night. Little did we know that Corey, at 37 years of age, would be killed the next day in a car wreck leaving behind his wife and two children. As a pastor, I had a grasp of the brevity of life and how precious it is, but it was through this experience that the Lord deepened that understanding. The greatest take-away from this heartbreaking event of losing my brother was a major sense of urgency for fully following Jesus and making His name known.

It was during this time that I really started to look inside myself to see who controlled my yes. Was it my family? Was it my church? Was it my friends? Was it the culture? If my yes really controlled my actions, then what was I going to do with this deeper sense of urgency?

This led me to think about the importance of last words. The last words I had with my brother were great. I have no regrets over the last time we spoke. They were full of love and kindness toward each other. They are words that I will hold on to for a lifetime. I realized that if the last words of my brother were that important to me, then the last words of Jesus should be even more important.

I began to grasp in a deeper way that if Jesus controls my yes, then His last words should seriously matter to me.

I went to the Great Commission in Matthew Chapter 28. It was there that Jesus' earthly presence was winding down and He was leaving last words with His followers to fuel them for the days to come. So, He said that they were to, *"Go and make disciples. Baptize them in the name of the Father, Son, and the Holy Spirit teaching them to obey all that I have commanded you. And lo, I am with you even to the end of the age."*

You see, Jesus was not only speaking to His disciples, but also to us. The question is not whether He is speaking. He is. The question is whether or not we are listening, heeding, and responding. If He controls our yes, then our actions should be to go across the street, the city, North America, and the world.

In His very last words before His ascension, recorded in Acts 1:8, Jesus calls us to be His *"witnesses in Jerusalem and in all Judea and Samaria and to the end of the earth."* I have experienced a lot of people in the church world who will say they have a heart for missions, but their actions simply do not show that to be true! They are not financially supporting missions or being a part of missions opportunities in their communities or around the world. They aren't actively engaged in sharing the gospel. You can't say that you have a heart for missions and a love for Jesus and then not be engaged in His work.

If people were to look at your life in this very moment, who would they say controls your yes? Get in the game. Get off the sideline. Ask the Lord to open your heart and to give you a sense of urgency for the lost and to see His name carried around the world. Get out of your comfort zone, which is exactly where Satan wants you to stay, and put your yes on the table and let Jesus control it for the rest of your life!

It is then, and only then, that we can truly do what Jesus said in Matthew 6, which is to "store up for yourselves treasures in heaven..."

> You can't say that you have a heart for missions and a love for Jesus and then not be engaged in His work.

CHAPTER 14
When It Looks Like It's Coming to an End

It was Geoffery Chaucer who coined the phrase, "All good things must end." You don't have to have lived long to know that his statement is true. As a matter of fact, many, if not all, things come to an end.

When I think about things that end, vacations come to mind. I know how excited I am when my vacation comes around. You travel to your destination, arrive at the hotel, condo, or house, unpack your suitcase, stock the kitchen and then you get to take a deep breath. You sit down and there is an entire week ahead of you to rest and enjoy. I also know how sad I am when we pull into the driveway at the end of vacation and we have an entire car to unload, clothes to wash and things to do to get ready for the grind of regular life and the next week at work.

Across the Southeastern United States, and especially in Alabama, there is great excitement as the college football season begins. Likewise, there is always a great disappointment and let down when the season comes to an end. Careers end, relationships end, and by the way, life ends.

We have to step back and ask ourselves the question, whose hand is actually on the wheel? Am I in control of my life? Am I following my own way? Or is God in control of this journey? Am I listening to His call and following His wisdom about what's happening in my life at that moment?

I have seen that God teaches us the most when we are in the middle of indecision and periods of questioning. He can lead us through the storms when it seems like things are coming to an end if we will take the time to listen to His voice and to seek His will. One of the things that God has taught me over time is that He is never trying to hide His will from us and that He is rarely early but never late. What a great truth to learn!

There was a time when it seemed like Doulos Partners was coming to an end. One Wednesday, late in our third year as a ministry, Susan called me at the office. She was closing out the books for the month and was getting ready to process checks for our partners. I could tell by the sound of her voice that something was bothering her and that we were about to have a hard conversation. She told me that there wasn't enough cash on hand to pay the partners in full and still have enough money left to cover the administrative costs for the month.

After giving me a couple of options, one of which was to only make a small partial payment to the partners, she asked me what I wanted her to do. I was at a place where I had to decide whether I was going to trust the Lord to provide or whether our time at Doulos Partners over. You see, any ministry that relies solely on the donations of others never knows if there will ever be another dollar that comes in your door.

In that moment, I was reminded that Doulos Partners was not ours. God started it and had sustained it to that point. It was His. With that, I told her to pay the partners in full. She reminded me that by doing that we wouldn't have the money to meet payroll or other administrative costs. And she was right. However, I felt like this was a test to see if we really trusted in God to provide. What followed that experience was amazing.

That very afternoon, $11,000 of donations came into our office. I called Susan and we both cried and celebrated. That was, at that point in the ministry, one of the largest deposits in any given week. On that Friday, I received a call from one of our board members that had been working on a $5,000 grant with a foundation to tell me that they had decided to give $10,000 instead. If you have had much experience in foundation requests you know how rare that is. Most of the time you receive much less than what you are asking for, certainly not more.

I called Susan and we celebrated again. We went through the weekend thinking and talking about all that the Lord had done, but He was not finished yet. On Monday evening, as we were lying down for bed, I received an e-mail from another board member. He was letting me know how the Lord had blessed him with the sale of a building. Because of this, he was putting a check in the mail to the ministry for $20,000. Within a matter of five days we went from strategizing about how to move forward with an empty bank account to having $41,000 cash on hand.

God taught me so much during that experience. When you listen to the voice of God and trust in Him, you can press forward with integrity and obedience even in the midst of your doubts and fears. We can find rest in and have the assurance of the truth that God is trustworthy in helping us to carry out what He has called us to do. We do not control when it ends or how it ends; He does. We just have to be obedient in walking out our faith in Him and His call on our lives.

I am certain that there is someone, as they read this very page, that is questioning how they can accomplish what the Lord has called them to do. You are doubting whether you can even move forward at all. Satan may even be tempting you to quit or to make some kind of change to God's plan for you. If God is calling you, even if you don't understand it all, He will provide what you need in order for you to carry out His will. For Doulos Partners, it was to provide the financial resources because of our willingness to step out in faith. I am thankful to the Lord that He had more days ahead for our ministry. However, I would have needed to be equally content if it would have been the end.

When you have your yes controlled by the Lord, you realize that even the end is in His hands. If the Lord is closing a chapter, we can totally have the confidence that He will open the door to the next one. Just because He ends the chapter, it doesn't mean the narrative is over. It just means that there is a new chapter to the story.

We so often circumvent the will of God. We sometimes get ahead of the Lord or we lag behind Him. In Matthew Chapter 14, Peter was quick to get out of the boat and walk on the water. I can only imagine how those first steps felt. Can you get your mind around what must have been going on inside of him to be doing something that flew in the face of nature?

Man is not made to walk on water and yet there in the middle of the wind and the waves, that is exactly what he was doing. He was participating in something that contradicted all logic. And yet we know the only way that he was able to do that was through the power of Jesus and by keeping his eyes on Him.

> **If we can trust Him with our eternity, we can trust Him with the things on this earth.**

However, as he took his eyes off of the Lord and began to see the waves around him, he started to sink. Such as it is with our lives. The Lord, as he did with Peter, calls to us to get out of the boat. He is the one who gives us the ability and power to "walk on the water."

He wants us to keep our eyes on Him as we stay faithful to His assignment for us until the very end. Let Him begin it, let Him sustain it, and according to His will, let Him be the one who ends it.

If we can trust Him with our eternity, we can trust Him with the things on this earth. Don't ever be afraid to take what seems to be a risk with the Lord, because at the end of the day, if it is Jesus who is calling, is there really any risk at all?

CHAPTER 15
The Power of One

Doulos Partners began with God assembling three individuals who had their yes on the table. He continues to add to the team people who are sold out to what He has in store for them, which greatly impacts us as a ministry. It is a beautiful picture of what God can do when we each one say yes to His call.

I saw this recently when we had a team in Jordan. Pastor K, one of the indigenous leaders, took us to the region of the Gadarenes. This is where the story from Mark Chapter 5 took place. Jesus and His disciples crossed the sea of Galilee and landed on the Southeastern tip of the lake. They came up the hill and were met by a man who was demon-possessed. When Jesus asked him his name, the response was "Legion, for we are many".

We know from history that a legion of soldiers is about 6,000 strong. Scholars conclude that this indicated that there were many demons, even into the thousands, that had taken control of this man. We found ourselves at the apex of this hill where Jesus would have been approached. The original Roman road was to our left that led to the tombs where the demon-possessed man would have lived. Scripture tells us that those in the city would bind him in chains but he was too strong and broke any shackles that restrained him. There is great power in the darkness.

However, Jesus came to this region to find Legion and set him free. As best we can tell, this is the only time that Jesus brought His ministry into this region of the world and it was for one man, Legion. Mark tells us that Jesus spoke and commanded the demons to come out of the man and they entered into a herd of pigs that ran down the hill and into the sea. You see, as powerful as the darkness was, it was no match for the power of the Son of God. This man was found sitting fully clothed and in his right mind. He had been saved. He had been set free.

The man wanted to go with Jesus. He asked to get in the boat with Him but was denied. Jesus had an assignment for the man whom He had just set free and it is the same one that He has for each of us. It was the assignment to go and give an account of what he had experienced. He was to tell what his life was like before meeting Jesus and then to tell about the forgiveness and transformation that he had experienced after. For this one man, his assignment was to go into the Decapolis, the ten cities, to share about what God had done. Obediently, he went. These ten cities are in present day Jordan, Syria, and Israel.

While we were standing there and reading the story from Mark, Pastor K said "I am a follower of Christ today because this one man, centuries before, who was healed of demon possession by the hand of Jesus, was faithful to go and to tell the story of the encounter he had with the Son of the living God and brought the gospel to the country of Jordan."

I was reminded again that there is great power in one person faithfully answering the call of God on their life. There are so many stories in scripture where God used one faithful, obedient person to be a part of the work to advance His Kingdom.

This book is a collection of stories just as the Bible is a collection of books. It includes the stories of the three founders and how God used each of us to start the ministry. It is the stories of board members, ministry partners, staff, and donors. It is the stories of indigenous leaders all over the world who are on the frontlines of ministry. These stories are not to make heroes out of the people that are named in this book, but to show what it looks like to be a fully devoted follower of Christ. We are but individuals who have been set free from our sin of unbelief and who have been called to a purpose; to share the reason for the hope that we have which is in Jesus Christ our Lord. These stories are written down solely to give an account of the work of God and to make much of Him.

Now, you are a now a part of this story. Because you have taken time to read about the lives of the people in this book you, whether you realize it or even like it, are now included in the narrative. If you are like me, as I have met these incredible men and women of faith and have heard their stories, I have a tendency to compare my story to theirs. But what a huge mistake that it is to put our lives up against someone else's.

Here is the sobering truth: the Lord *never* judges us based on another person's call or assignment. He only holds us accountable to the one that He has given each one of us!

You see, you must come to the realization that God has a call and a purpose for *your* life. What are you going to do about that reality? Is your yes on the table?

You can make a difference, not only in this world, but for all of eternity. I implore you, just as Jesus did, to go and make disciples. To be salt and light in this dark and tasteless world. To be faithful to the call of Jesus and to be His witnesses in Jerusalem, Judea, Samaria, and the ends of the earth. Let me end this entire experience with one question, if the advancement of the gospel was left only in your hands, would it go forward? One person with one word, YES!!

> Here is the sobering truth: the Lord never judges us based on another person's call or assignment.

AFTERWORD
A Personal Note from David

The path in Michigan where David and Susan walked and talked
about the new call that would become Doulos Partners.

I have found that when the Lord calls you to serve in
His Kingdom, He often includes the entire family. This
has certainly been true for the Johnsons over the years
and His directive to start Doulos Partners was no
exception.

The three most important people in my life were, as you might have expected, the first to know about my 2:32 a.m. meeting with Jesus. I decided to go back and talk with them about their memories of how all this got started. They are my wife, Susan, our son, Brian, and our daughter, Bethany.

Brian was the first person to hear about what God had done. That morning, after my encounter with the Lord, my day started just like any other, even though I was still trying to put together all that He had revealed to me. By the afternoon, I decided to take a short break and call Brian to touch base. He lived in Michigan at the time and our frequent phone conversations helped us stay connected in spite of the miles between us. It was really not intentional on my part for him to be the first to know about what had happened but it just kind of ended up that way.

He recalled standing in the dining hall of the Young Life camp at Timberwolf Lake Lodge when my call came. I told him everything that the Lord had said to me and we discussed the differences between micro and macro ministry. Brian remembered the excitement I had for this new season even though it was unclear of all that the Lord was calling me to do. That phone call ended with a time of dreaming together about what it could mean for the future and we both came away from our talk looking forward to the ride that God had for us.

Beginning with our discussion over dinner that night, Susan and I had many conversations about the "wake me up in the middle of the night" moment. After 42 years of marriage, she has learned to take the major twists and turns God has placed in our path in stride. The most significant moment that she remembered vividly happened late in 2007, after the meetings with John, Wayne and Scott.

We had traveled to Michigan to celebrate Thanksgiving with our family. On Thanksgiving morning, we woke up to a winter wonderland. As we walked in the snow along some beautiful paths around the camp, we talked about what this new assignment would mean for our family, our church, and our direction. There was an enthusiasm about what God was doing even though those feelings were also mixed with an uncertainty of the future. We were both sure that we had a fresh call from the Lord, just like the fresh fallen snow that surrounded us. More importantly, there was a firm commitment, a yes on the table, for whatever He had for us to do.

In our wildest dreams we could not have scripted the journey that God would give us to travel.

It has certainly been one filled with adventure and we are so excited about the new roads that He has for us to explore in the future.

Bethany told me that her first recollection of the changes that we were considering came from her mom. As most mothers do, Susan called to make sure Bethany was up to date on all that was taking place with the possible new directive that God had given us. Bethany remembered her first reaction to that call was FEAR.

One of the many things that I love about Bethany is that she does not mince words or hold in her feelings. She went on to say that her fear was for my safety as I would more than likely be traveling to places that were dangerous. She was also afraid of the financial risk that came from leaving a stable position at a growing church and moving into the unknown, which also did not surprise me. She is one of the most financially responsible people and best money managers that I know. A gift, that anyone who knows our family well, understands she got from her mom. The cool part for me is, she said even with those fears, there was a peace that came over her because of the trust she felt in us as we were following the Lord to the best of our ability. Wow, what a vote of confidence!

One of the many things that we have been able to see over the last ten years has been the faithfulness of God to give His protection in the field and for His provision for not only Susan and me, but Doulos as well. The Lord has certainly been our provider and our protector.

To write a book is not something that happens every day. As a matter of fact, most people will never have this opportunity. Since this is my first, and more than likely my last, I want to give a word to my children, grandchildren, and should Jesus tarry, even to those future generations in our family.

First, to Susan, words cannot begin express what the journey has been like for me being your husband. You have been an incredible helpmate to me in EVERY way. Many of you have heard me say that if you look up "helpmate" in the dictionary, her picture is there. That may not be true in reality, but it is certainly true in practice. You have been such a blessing to me. When I find myself in tough situations, next to the Lord, your voice is the one ringing in my ears. The unconditional love and support that you have shown has been the fuel that has allowed me to do what the Lord has called me to do over all these years. The way that you have worked tirelessly side by side with me at Doulos has been amazing.

You are, in every way, a Proverbs 31 woman. I love you so much and appreciate you and the way that we have gotten to lead our family together and to go through life arm in arm. The Lord could not have chosen a more perfect woman for me than you. Thank you for saying yes!

To Brian and Bethany, even though it has not always been easy and without challenges, next to being your mom's husband, the thing that has brought me the greatest joy is getting to be your dad. Watching you grow up and become the man and woman that you are today has been amazing to watch. The way that you love, respect, serve, and meet the needs of your mates is God-honoring and heart-warming. I am also pleased to see how you are raising your children in the fear and admonition of the Lord. DON'T STOP!!!

Let me state the obvious here. You are raising our grandchildren in the most difficult time that I have ever seen in our country and in our world. If they are going to be prepared to face all that Satan and his demons are going to throw their way, you guys are going to have to continue to teach them how to put on the WHOLE armor of God. Also, you two are next generation leaders for the advancement of the kingdom. Take that responsibility seriously!

Mom and I have worked so hard to lay a foundation that God can build on and my challenge to you is to be reckless in your following of Jesus. Eternity hangs in the balance and my prayer is that our example will be one that you guys embrace to make Jesus' name known around the world. I love you both so much and I am so proud of you!

Let me say a word to our other two children, Brad Timothy (Bethany's husband) and Christy Johnson (Brian's wife). Susan and I prayed for you, even though we did not know you yet, standing over Brian and Bethany's cribs when they were just babies. We asked the Lord to send our children Godly mates. In His mercy and grace, He did just that. Both of you have been such a joy to us and a great part of our family. So many times "in-laws" are "out-laws." That is certainly not the case with the two of you. From the time of saying "I do," you both have joined right in with our crazy clan. Thank you for loving and being devoted to our kids. Thank you for bringing us grandkids and for the way that you are raising them. Thank you for being a part of Doulos by giving, going, praying, and supporting us as we carry out our call from the Lord. Susan and I love you so much and we are so grateful that you are a part of our family.

To Jocelyn, Annabelle, Piper Joy, Eby, and Hutch: ZuZu and PeePaw love you so much. We pray for each one of you every day and we know that God has a purpose and a plan for your lives. When Jesus was asked what the greatest commandment was He said, "love God and love people." Kids, don't miss this! Jesus is saying this is the most important thing. It is to be at the core of who we are and what we do as a Christ-follower. You see, as our relationship deepens with God, our love and concern for others grows deeper and wider. It is out of that love that other people matter more than ourselves. It is out of that love that we can help others come to know Jesus as their

Savior. As much as I know you love your families, and I am so thankful for that, the most important love and devotion must be to Jesus. So, read your Bibles every day, pray, help those in need, stay intimately connected to a strong body of true believers, and share the gospel everywhere you go. If you will remember these words and put them into practice, your lives will matter for the Kingdom, which is all that we could ever ask for! One last thing, just as ZuZu and PeePaw prayed for those who were going to marry our kids, we are praying for the one that God has chosen for you and the families that He is going to give you.

The pages of this book are not to celebrate me or my family. God used us to advance His Kingdom not because we are special or significant, but because we were willing to say yes. My desire is that this book will be like the stones set up in Joshua Chapter 4. I pray that when my grandchildren, great grandchildren and even great, great grandchildren pick up this book years from now, they will point to it as a memorial stone of what God has done so that *"...all the peoples of the earth may know that the hand of the Lord is mighty, that you may fear the Lord, your God forever." Joshua 4:24*

What's Next?

Now that you have heard the Doulos story, we want to invite you to join us in what God is doing in and through Doulos Partners! Here are four ways that you, your business, your family or church can begin to be a part of Kingdom building around the world.

1) **Invest Monthly** – Although we receive many one-time gifts, the monthly commitments of our partners allow us to keep financial commitments to our national missionaries on the ground. They also allow us to plan and execute expansions in current countries as well as into new countries. We are asking you to make a monthly pledge and to start giving your monthly donation as soon as possible!

2) **Leverage Relationships** – Invite some of your missional friends to a gathering in your office or home and allow a Doulos presentation to be done. You could also arrange a meeting at a coffee shop or local restaurant with a missional friend or colleague so that our Founder & CEO, President, or other Doulos representatives can share the Doulos story.

3) **Prayer & Fasting** – One of the many impressive things about our national missionaries is the fervency of their prayer lives. We realize that without prayer and obedience to the word that our ministry is powerless. Please commit to pray over both the domestic and international efforts of Doulos.

4) **Disciple Making** – Jesus said, five days before His ascension, "Therefore go and make disciples of all nations, baptizing them in the name of the Father and of the Son and of the Holy Spirit and teaching them to obey everything I have commanded you. And surely I am with you always, to the very end of the age." Prayerfully consider accompanying us on one of our trips to the field. As you go, in obedience to God's word, you can be assured that the Lord will change your life forever.

www.doulospartners.org